DESIGNING WITH THE WOOL

Advanced Techniques In Navajo Weaving

DESIGNING
WITH THE
WOOL

Advanced Techniques
In Navajo Weaving

NOËL BENNETT

NORTHLAND PRESS / FLAGSTAFF

In the spirit of

RUTH WILLOUGHBY KENNY   1821–1909
ISABELLE KENNY SMITH   1859–1938
RUTH SMITH MEYER-GIELOW   1885
MERTON MEYER KIRKISH   1910

*each of whom wove on their own warp
in search of their own Truths.*

Contents

List of Illustrations

Introduction

DEEP IN SHADOW the woman stood motionless — dark hair, dark skin, dark eyes heightening obscurity. Across her velvet blouse arms folded tightly. Beneath her satin skirt feet were planted firmly. I found myself there before her, feeling as an intruder, and suddenly quite unsure as to why I had ever come.

"You're here on an important mission," I reprimanded myself, impatient at my sudden reticence. "This is your chance to find someone to teach you to weave!"

Navajo weaving! Here was a beauty I felt strongly drawn toward. Here was a process I urgently wanted to learn and to integrate within. My physician–husband, just out of internship, had joined the Public Health Service. We were in Tuba City, Arizona, on the Navajo Reservation. This was my chance — if only I could find someone to teach me.

"She speaks good English," the words from the day before rang in my ears. It was Clara, her daughter-in-law, who had assured me. "She speaks good English. You ask her," she had prodded. And so, clinging to this encouragement I had come now to pose the question.

To look at her at this moment was to disbelieve she spoke at all. Her expression was neither one of welcome nor unwelcome. I estimated her age somewhere in the early fifties — and yet she seemed ageless. Clara had said she would ask first. Had she forgotten? Or had she asked and the weaver said "No"? Again I looked to the face for an answer, but the expression lent no cause for hope.

The hogan behind was hand-hewn of cedar and lovely. The earth beneath was red and hard where many feet had trod. The curious expressions

1

of her children and grandchildren now fronted a circle — staring at the stranger who had unexpectedly appeared in their camp.

Trying to formulate the words, I reasoned my alternatives. She looked too traditional to speak English. Of course, if this were so, words would be useless anyway, I reminded myself. On the other hand, suppose she *did* speak English and Clara *had* asked her. Well, then she would already know why I had come, and again words would be superfluous. A smile seemed the only remaining course of action.

It was a difficult smile to find and slow in coming. But this time as I looked up, the shadowy visage cleared, revealing a nicely featured face — not particularly friendly, but not unfriendly either. And most of all it was a wise and clear face. I felt my smile broaden.

For whatever time the situation required, I awaited her response. And it came. It came with a change of expression, a shift of weight, and then a crossing of the well-trodden path to a nearby corral. With economy of motion, she reached forth removing a sheepskin that hung casually over the rail. And by that simple gesture a shimmering of golds, browns and rusts — like the sun, earth and bodies themselves — were brought to life. Her weaving rose unveiled before me.

It was a textural masterpiece, the whole. Even. Clear-featured. Definitive. Like the weaver herself. I stepped forward to admire. My fingertips scanned the surface. I could feel the lanolin of the raw wool and the rhythmic joints perfected from years of repetition.

"It's beautiful!" I blurted out. "Clara said you were a good weaver and you are!" It was an impulsive, spontaneous reaction. It was a statement of pure fact. The kind requiring no reply. But an answer came nonetheless. It was spoken after the proper period of silence, and haltingly by one unsure of the English vocabulary.

"I should be," she said. "I've been weaving since I was seven."

Such was my introduction to Tiana Bighorse: halting, unsure, but positive. And later, when I *could* find the words to ask if she would teach me, her reply was equally to the point: "How long do you have to learn?" she stated.

Knowing that the family would be in Tuba City for at least two years, there seemed no need for further thought. But I waited my proper period of silence, trying to repress the confidence I felt toward the answer to follow.

I formulated the simplest, least embellished response: "Two years."

But her clouded expression did not change and I found myself quickly and unexpectedly adding, "Will that be enough?"

Eyes were shifted down. Lips were still. The transitive expression that had clouded her face had vanished and her face was void once again. She had returned to her former position encased in hogan shadows. Eternity lapsed before I received the considered reply: "Perhaps."

It has been nine years since that meeting day. Many times I have relived those moments, recalling her economical choice of words. They were uttered by one who had been weaving for half a century to a stranger just wanting to undertake the craft. And with the passing of time I have come to further understand their truth; two years has *not* been enough.

During the years 1967–76 Tiana Bighorse was one of many weavers who took me underwing to teach me Navajo weaving and Navajo way. In fact, during the family's time in and around the reservation, about twenty different women made their rounds — checking on The Doctor's Wife That Weaves — patiently showing, correcting, advising. At one point Tiana Bighorse mentioned she had always wanted to learn the diamond twill. Surprised that a weaver of her competence didn't know the method, I inquired. Her answer echoed what other weavers had already said: The Navajo are "stingy" with their knowledge.

The concept of "stinginess" is quite understandable when one considers the context. In this culture of unwritten language, knowledge is selectively handed down, difficult to come by, highly prized. Not available from books, learning can be acquired only by apprenticing to one who knows and is willing to impart. This is generally possible only from a close relative and at great personal expense. Additionally, since "to teach" means "to show," and words of instruction are few, much perseverance and dedication are required of the learner. Under this system, it takes years to obtain any real understanding, and once acquired, this hard-earned body of knowledge — now a form of power — is in turn not freely given.

Tiana Bighorse had always wanted to learn the diamond twill. Since it was not in her mother's repertoire, the technique was not passed along in her "formal weaving instruction." There *was* an aunt, however, who could weave that way. On several occasions Tiana Bighorse had visited her and indicated an interest in learning. On one occasion, she had even been permitted to watch her weave. But the process was complicated and not evident from the surface — and naturally her aunt never offered an explanation! On another occasion she again broached the subject of learning, only to have a cousin intervene with the suggestion: "Make her give you all her jewelry and *then* show her how!"

"So," Tiana Bighorse concluded, "I never learned."

Needless to say, when I offered to show her both the diamond twill and the two-faced, she was an avid learner and her appreciation was obvious. To her, it was a fulfillment of a lifelong wish. And I was only too glad to put something back into the reservoir from which I had so constantly drawn.

3

Years have passed. Friendships and trusts have strengthened. Together our dreams have budded and blossomed. What started as a wish to preserve Navajo weaving techniques for younger-generation Navajo girls has far exceeded our expectations. In 1971 Tiana Bighorse and I co-authored *Working with the Wool: How to Weave a Navajo Rug.* Since that time the book has been reprinted seven times, and its use is now widespread: in reservation boarding schools, at Navajo Community College, at the University of New Mexico in Gallup, and well beyond. It is with great satisfaction to both of us that we have seen weaving circles and universities throughout the country recognize the beauty of Navajo weaving and identify with the process.

Growing out of such widespread interest, *Designing with the Wool* has now come to be — focusing on the advanced techniques of Navajo weaving. Recorded here for kindred weavers to whom "two years has also not been enough," the techniques are offered to Navajo and non-Navajo alike. And if in the taking and using of them, they are accorded half the appreciation, half the dedication, half the recognition of their value as shown by Tiana Bighorse at *her* moment of learning, then my efforts in collecting and recording will once again have been very well rewarded.

CHAPTER 1

Take Stock

THIS IS A BOOK FOR WEAVERS who have fallen in love with Navajo weaving. Perhaps it was the organic nature of the craft that first took your fancy — the use of found wood to scavenge the loom, the hunting of the perfect tree branch to shape your batten or fork. Perhaps you enjoy philosophy and have discovered that here is an art form strongly rooted in culture, rich in lore, ritual and life-wisdom. Or perhaps you simply consider Navajo weaving to be the most satisfying way to explore and preserve the lovely patterns your mind's eye holds.

Whatever the lure, whatever the beauty, by now you've probably woven a few basic projects with varying degrees of success. Moreover, while others have dropped by the wayside in frustration, you find that the challenge of this craft only urges you onward, feeding your energy and providing you with additional eagerness. The question in your mind at this point is not, "Shall I do another?" Rather it is, "Where do I go from here?"

A quick perusal of Navajo rugs reveals a virtually unlimited scope. Many types of weaving can be done on your simple loom, the main limitation being the weaver's imagination and skill. It is to both of these areas that this book has been directed. I hope the designs and ideas provide you with inspiration. I hope, too, that the directions are basic enough to produce competent results you can be proud of.*

---

*Directions may occasionally refer you back to *Working With the Wool* for additional clarification. In these instances the text initials (WWW) and page numbers will be given.

Trouble-shooting

In answering the question, "Where do I go from here?" it is necessary to consider first, "Where am I now?" To this end I have prepared some questions to help you take stock of your present state, to evaluate your past projects. Included, too, are some suggestions for improvement. With your weavings before you and in an objective, reminiscent frame of mind, consider the following:

I. *How was your warping?*

A. Was your warp evenly tensioned clear across your weaving? OR were there sections of softly and tightly strung warp?

The time to check and remedy your warp is when you have it mounted on your loom, right after heddles have been made. First be certain that the warp is absolutely vertical. Then feel the tension across your warp, pressing with fingers. If one section is looser than the rest tighten it as follows:

Working from the tight section to the loose section, pull each consecutive front warp firmly and evenly to take up slack — clear across the warp. (If you are working from left to right, pull UP on each warp the stick-shed holds forward. If working from right to left, pull DOWN on each warp the stick-shed holds forward.) Repeat the process as necessary until all warps feel the same when your fingers press against them. Then retie the end knot.

B. Knots

If you had trouble with warp knots slipping during the weaving, we suggest you try the bowline. Though initially more complicated than the square, it produces a knot that will not slip under tension or fork action. Directions for the bowline follow. It may be necessary to practice it before applying it to your weaving.

The bowline knot is used at the beginning of your warp and again at the end. It is also especially good in repairing a broken warp. As pictured in Figure 1, make a kink in the warp before circling the dowel. Visualize the kink as a "hole" at a bottom of a tree, the strand above as the "trunk," and the end as a "rabbit." Be certain that in making the hole, the warp-end crosses over both "tree trunk" and dowel.

Having circled the dowel (Fig. 1.1), repeat to yourself: "Rabbit goes UP THROUGH hole, AROUND BEHIND the tree, and BACK DOWN into the hole." Then thread warp end as shown above (Fig. 1.2), and tighten evenly.

In the instance that the knot need be tied under tension (i.e. the final warp knot or a warp-repair knot), threading is still done with slack yarn. It is the tightening which adjusts the tension and can be accomplished by pulling

6

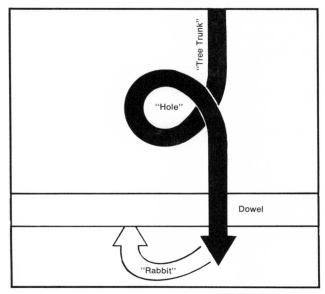

Figure 1.1: *Preliminary looping of the bowline knot.*

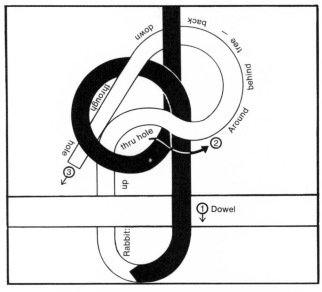

Figure 1.2: *Final threading of the bowline knot.*

7

each strand in the direction and in the order indicated above in Figure 2.

1. Pull DOWN on strand going over dowel. (This will tighten the "hole.") Hold tightened hole between thumb and index finger of left hand and then . . .
2. Pull UP on right strand above hole until tension is as desired.
3. Pull DOWN on end of warp to anchor knot and preserve tension.

II. *What yarns did you use? Were they appropriate to the piece?*

Warp for Navajo weaving should be fine and strong. It should be able to withstand the tension of the loom and the abrasion of fork and heddle action. Some elasticity is desirable and 100% wool is definitely preferred. When spacing your warp, consider the use the piece will receive. The heavier the wear, the larger the warp-spacing should be. Finer tapestries, conversely, require closer spacing. Three settings will cover most needs:

6 warps/ inch (3 marks/inch on dowel) for heavy floor rug.

8 warps/inch (4 marks/inch on dowel) for all-purpose work.

(This is the generally recommended setting.)

12 warps/inch (6 marks/inch on dowel) for finer tapestries or in 4-shed techniques where packing is pronounced.

Weft also has requirements. The Navajo sheep fleece is fine and short fibered. Spun on the Navajo spindle, the result is a soft, fluffy, almost matted yarn with surprising elasticity and strength.

Good Navajo weavers try for an exacting warp/weft ratio whereby the wool fibers interlock. Weft that is too fine for the warp spacing overpacks. Not only does the weaving go interminably slowly, but excessive packing crushes each weft down upon the last with detriment to the lovely texture of the handspun. On the other hand, weft that is too thick or overspun cannot be beaten down sufficiently and therefore leaves warps exposed. Ideally, each row of packed weft should fully settle around the warp base to give complete coverage, yet be held up, one upon the other, so each strand can be seen and appreciated separately.

III. *How was your packing? How was your warp spacing?*

Did your weft completely cover your warp?

Did your warps stay evenly spaced throughout?

OR did warps ease together so that weft built up in tight areas and refused to beat down with the rest of the row?

Close warps usually indicate that you are not putting enough weft in each row; your scallops are not big enough. Try making five scallops, instead of four across the ten-inch weaving. Keep them the same height as before. Remember that you want a *tight warp* but a *relaxed weft!* Think loose! Learn to view a little surface rippling of the yarn as a thing of beauty.

8

Watch your warp spacing carefully. You might hang a dark cloth behind the weaving so warp spacing is clearly discernible. As soon as warps start to ease together take immediate and decisive action:

1. Take out a few rows to ease the problem.
2. Redistribute the warps *with authority!* (p. 85 WWW)
3. Fill in the valleys with weft (p. 84 WWW) calmly and in a matter-of-fact manner. Remember that even good Navajo weavers use fill-ins almost every third row! Fill-ins are a fact of life.
4. Resume weaving, putting more weft into the shed as described above.

IV. *How are your joints? How are your side loops?*

Are your joints between colors smooth and flat?
Are your side loops regular and firm?
OR are all your designs outlined with ridges?
Are your side loops floppy, oversized and irregular?

Ridges at joints and oversized side loops are the result of not pulling yarn tightly enough at that particular spot. To prevent pulling so hard that warps are displaced, however, try this approach:

1. After inserting weft into shed, pull it *securely* around the warp or joint.
2. Using your fingers, press the joint or loop down into place.
3. *Then* lay the yarn in *loosely* for the rest of the row.

Pressing the joint down after the initial tight tug will make crisp, flat joints. Since joints occur mid-row, it will be necessary to reach through the warp to grasp the joint between index finger and thumb.

V. *How is your finishing end?*

When your rug is folded in half, are both ends of equal width?
Is the finishing end smooth and well-packed?
OR is the top end significantly narrower?
Is it roughly woven with warp showing through the weft?

There is no doubt that finishing the rug is the most tedious part of the whole. One can only take heart by reminding oneself that Navajo weavers have done it beautifully for years and that what is begun in beauty should also be finished in beauty. To make certain that the top end will be as wide as the bottom, measure the warp once on the loom and force top warps outward to compensate for the one less mark on the top dowel. On the *Working with the Wool* project, top and bottom should both equal 10¼". Again when about 3" from the top, remeasure in case warps have eased back together during the weaving process.

As for smooth texture, there is no replacement for patience. Slowly and painstakingly thread your weft through the warp with the sacking needle, being careful *not to split warps or cross weft.* Blunt the needle point if necessary. The rewards of a patient completion are self-evident and bountiful!

Where do I go from here?

Where you go from here depends on how you've done so far and how pleased you are with your results. Here are some suggestions for future projects. Each possibility receives full treatment within the book.

I. *If you have completed a striped rug and would like to begin working in design:*

Follow the directions for the project given in *Working with the Wool.*

II. *If you have completed a design project with hooked joints and would like to work further on smoothing out your ridges:*

A. Turn to Chapter 2. You will find several designs charted which use the hooked joint and which stay with the same 10″ x 23″ warping dimensions.

B. Like that idea but wish your weaving were a bit wider? Consider warping 3 marks/inch on the dowel instead of 4. 40 warps will yield 13⅓″ width instead of 10″. Just remember to choose a heavier weft and to buy a bit more. However, your design count will remain exactly the same as charted.

C. Rather weave your own design? Turn to Chapter 9, which provides directions for charting. A formula for computing quantities of warp and weft will help you with yarn purchases.

III. *Maybe you have completed small hooked joint projects and would like to experiment with a larger weaving.*

How does 20″ x 40″ sound? To keep your interest and provide you with challenge, plan to use *triple* edging and selvage cords (p. 92 WWW) which create beautiful bindings along the edges and six tasseled corners. Choose one of the designs in Chapter 2 that gives you experience with a border. Since these are charted 10″ x 20″ and your weaving will be twice as long and wide, you will simply use twice as many warps in each design area and continue that design twice as long. Chapter 5 will give you full directions on converting your loom to accommodate warp that is longer than the height of your loom.

IV. *So you've only worked with the hooked joint and would like to try your hand with the turned?*

I refer you to Chapter 3. Here directions and charting have been done to give you experience in making smooth diagonal designs — a most useful skill.

V. *Perhaps you want to jump in completely, trying everything at once?*

Then the sampler is for you. Combining seven advanced techniques into a lovely whole, this weaving incorporates tufting, the turned joint, Coal Mine raised edge, small and medium diamond twills, pictorial, Crystal and two-faced!

VI. *Already done a sampler and are still hungry?*

    A. Try combining hooked and turned joints in the same rug (Chapter 4).
    B. Or make a *big loom* and do a *big rug* (Chapter 5).
    C. Always wanted to do a two-faced? Let Chapter 8 and the two-faced diamond twill fill your hours! Or take a deep breath and plunge into the "Morning Star" design which uses two-faced techniques exclusively.

Whatever your experience, whatever your ambition — there's a beautiful weaving ahead for you!

CHAPTER 2

Perfect the Hooked Joint

IF YOU ARE ENJOYING the rhythm of the hooked joint,* or if you are contemplating a durable weaving in which the strength of the hooked joint is appealing, you might look to some of the following designs as a next project. Each is designed with vertical lines exclusively. Each has warp and weft computed. Design counts and warping dimensions are also recorded.

The "Greek Key"

The scrollwork in this design is a favorite among weavers of all areas of the reservation. As drawn in Figure 2.1, it is the simplest of this section. However, it can be easily enlarged to provide varying degrees of complexity. Ideas for enlargement are included (see Figures 2.2, 2.3 and 2.4).

Two Grey Hills

The Two Grey Hills area of the reservation is heralded for its fine tapestry weave. Rugs are characterized by subtlety of color — only natural fleece hues being used. As such these rugs are easy to live with and there is less fading of color with exposure to light. Two different patterns are drawn in Figures 2.5 and 2.6, the second a bit more difficult than the first.

*Also called "interlocking weft" (see pp. 62–70, WWW).

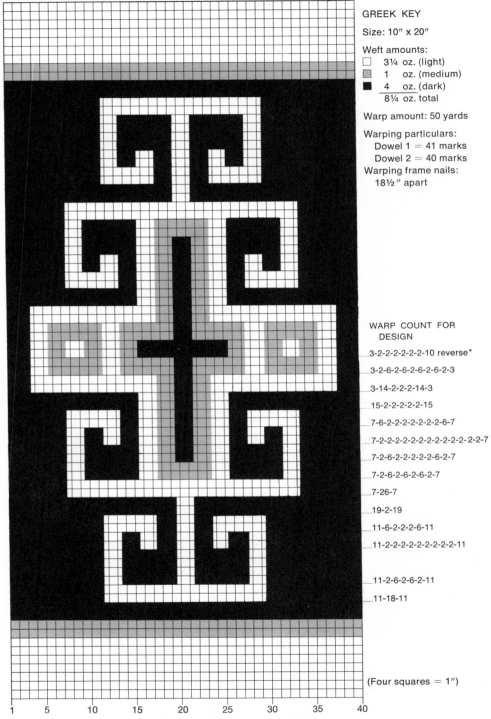

GREEK KEY

Size: 10″ x 20″

Weft amounts:
- ☐ 3¼ oz. (light)
- ▨ 1 oz. (medium)
- ■ 4 oz. (dark)
  - 8¼ oz. total

Warp amount: 50 yards

Warping particulars:
  Dowel 1 = 41 marks
  Dowel 2 = 40 marks
Warping frame nails:
  18½″ apart

WARP COUNT FOR
DESIGN

3-2-2-2-2-2-2-10 reverse*

3-2-6-2-6-2-6-2-6-2-3

3-14-2-2-2-14-3

15-2-2-2-2-2-15

7-6-2-2-2-2-2-2-6-7

7-2-2-2-2-2-2-2-2-2-2-2- 2-2-7

7-2-6-2-2-2-2-2-6-2-7

7-2-6-2-6-2-6-2-7

7-26-7

19-2-19

11-6-2-2-2-6-11

11-2-2-2-2-2-2-2-2-2-11

11-2-6-2-6-2-11

11-18-11

(Four squares = 1″)

Figure 2.1: *Greek Key design charted.*

The Greek Key design drawn in Figure 2.1 may be enlarged in several ways.

1. A solid 2¼″ border around the project will give you a 15″ x 20″ size (Fig. 2.2). Be aware that this increases the difficulty of the project, as you will have to maintain the border-vertical, in the same spot, for the entire length.

Figure 2.2: *Greek Key variation: plain border.*

2. Doubling the width, and thus the warp counts, will give you a squarer 20″ x 20″ look (Fig. 2.3). There would be no side border to maintain with this design.

Figure 2.3: *Greek Key variation: expanded design.*

3. For the ambitious already-accomplished weaver who seeks further challenge, a large patterned border (Fig. 2.4) will provide hours of enjoyment and concentration! Remember here that the finishing end will be difficult, with so much pattern present.

Figure 2.4: *Greek Key variation: ornate border.*

14

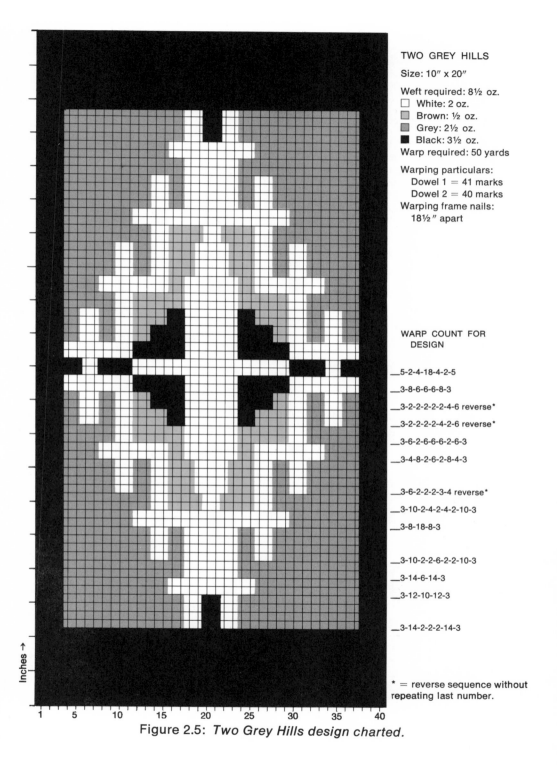

TWO GREY HILLS

Size: 10″ x 20″

Weft required: 8½ oz.
☐ White: 2 oz.
▨ Brown: ½ oz.
▦ Grey: 2½ oz.
■ Black: 3½ oz.
Warp required: 50 yards

Warping particulars:
   Dowel 1 = 41 marks
   Dowel 2 = 40 marks
Warping frame nails:
   18½″ apart

WARP COUNT FOR
DESIGN

__5-2-4-18-4-2-5

__3-8-6-6-6-8-3

__3-2-2-2-2-2-4-6 reverse*

__3-2-2-2-2-4-2-6 reverse*

__3-6-2-6-6-6-2-6-3

__3-4-8-2-6-2-8-4-3

__3-6-2-2-2-3-4 reverse*

__3-10-2-4-2-4-2-10-3

__3-8-18-8-3

__3-10-2-2-6-2-2-10-3

__3-14-6-14-3

__3-12-10-12-3

__3-14-2-2-2-14-3

* = reverse sequence without
repeating last number.

Inches →

1   5   10   15   20   25   30   35   40

Figure 2.5: *Two Grey Hills design charted.*

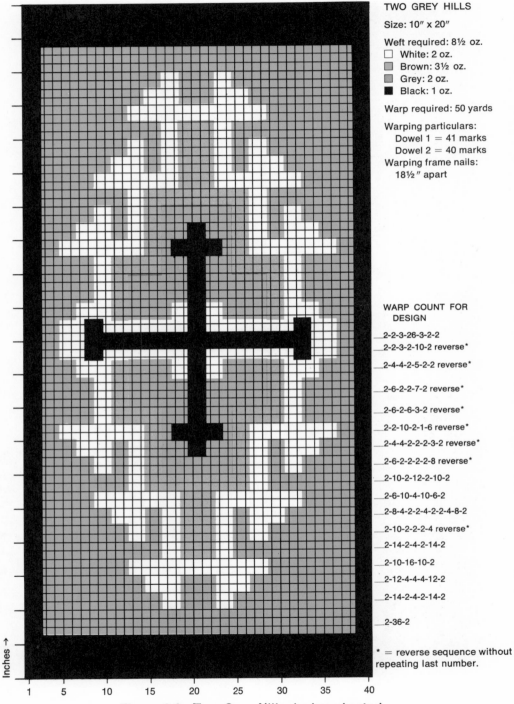

TWO GREY HILLS

Size: 10″ x 20″

Weft required: 8½ oz.
☐ White: 2 oz.
▨ Brown: 3½ oz.
▨ Grey: 2 oz.
■ Black: 1 oz.

Warp required: 50 yards

Warping particulars:
 Dowel 1 = 41 marks
 Dowel 2 = 40 marks
Warping frame nails:
 18½″ apart

WARP COUNT FOR
DESIGN

__2-2-3-26-3-2-2
__2-2-3-2-10-2 reverse*
__2-4-4-2-5-2-2 reverse*

__2-6-2-2-7-2 reverse*

__2-6-2-6-3-2 reverse*

__2-2-10-2-1-6 reverse*

__2-4-4-2-2-2-3-2 reverse*

__2-6-2-2-2-2-8 reverse*

__2-10-2-12-2-10-2

__2-6-10-4-10-6-2

__2-8-4-2-2-4-2-2-4-8-2

__2-10-2-2-2-4 reverse*

__2-14-2-4-2-14-2

__2-10-16-10-2

__2-12-4-4-4-12-2

__2-14-2-4-2-14-2

__2-36-2

* = reverse sequence without
repeating last number.

Inches →

1 5 10 15 20 25 30 35 40

Figure 2.6: *Two Grey Hills design charted.*

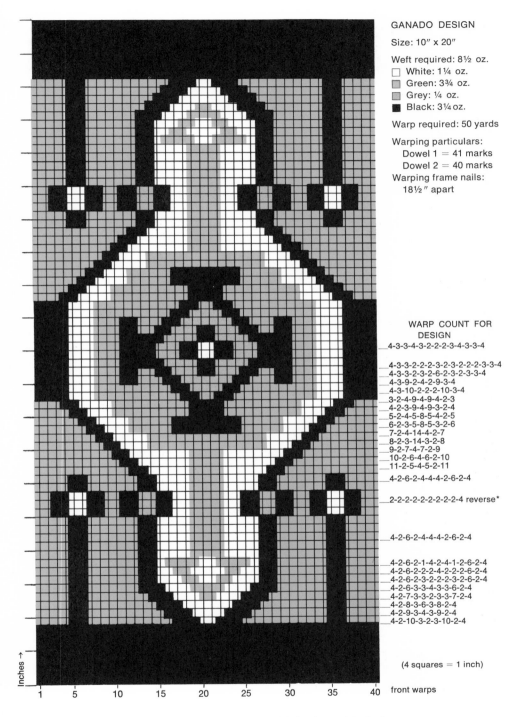

GANADO DESIGN

Size: 10″ x 20″

Weft required: 8½ oz.
☐ White: 1¼ oz.
▨ Green: 3¾ oz.
▨ Grey: ¼ oz.
■ Black: 3¼ oz.

Warp required: 50 yards

Warping particulars:
  Dowel 1 = 41 marks
  Dowel 2 = 40 marks
Warping frame nails:
  18½″ apart

WARP COUNT FOR
DESIGN
4-3-3-4-3-2-2-2-3-4-3-3-4

4-3-3-2-2-2-3-2-3-2-2-2-3-3-4
4-3-3-2-3-2-6-2-3-2-3-3-4
4-3-9-2-4-2-9-3-4
4-3-10-2-2-2-10-3-4
3-2-4-9-4-9-4-2-3
4-2-3-9-4-9-3-2-4
5-2-4-5-8-5-4-2-5
6-2-3-5-8-5-3-2-6
7-2-4-14-4-2-7
8-2-3-14-3-2-8
9-2-7-4-7-2-9
10-2-6-4-6-2-10
11-2-5-4-5-2-11

4-2-6-2-4-4-4-2-6-2-4

2-2-2-2-2-2-2-2-2-4 reverse*

4-2-6-2-4-4-4-2-6-2-4

4-2-6-2-1-4-2-4-1-2-6-2-4
4-2-6-2-2-4-2-2-2-6-2-4
4-2-6-2-3-2-2-2-3-2-6-2-4
4-2-6-3-3-4-3-3-6-2-4
4-2-7-3-3-2-3-3-7-2-4
4-2-8-3-6-3-8-2-4
4-2-9-3-4-3-9-2-4
4-2-10-3-2-3-10-2-4

(4 squares = 1 inch)

Inches →

1   5   10   15   20   25   30   35   40   front warps

Figure 2.7: *Ganado design charted.*

Ganado

In the center of the reservation is another fine weaving area: Ganado. The developing trend here has been toward rugs with deep rich red, produced by dyeing yarn double strength with aniline dye (specifically, "Cardinal Red"). The pattern in Figure 2.7 is the most difficult in this section.

Other designs

When drawing your own designs to be used with the hooked joint, place vertical design edges *between* warps — just like yarns hook. If you would prefer to use the turned joint with these designs, you can redraw them placing the vertical design edges *on* the warp. Additional information for the latter is given in the turned-warp chapter, and specific instruction for both in Chapter 8.

CHAPTER 3

Try the Turned Joint

THE TURNED JOINT is known by a variety of names — among them "shared warp," and "interlocking warp." Though sometimes used as an alternative to the hooked joint in making vertical lines, many weavers dislike the build-up that occurs, especially if the design is prolonged, as in a border.

Perhaps its best feature comes to fore in rendering a smooth diagonal line, as in the diamond pictured in Figure 3.1.

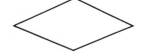

Figure 3.1:
Smooth diamond shape.

General concept

I. *The turning warp*

In the turned joint there is no hooking of wefts. Instead, two wefts will turn around and thus share the same "turning warp" (Fig. 3.2).

Figure 3.2: *Two wefts circling a turning warp.*

II. *Charting the turned joint*

When you are charting a turned joint design, just draw all vertical design edges ON a vertical ruling of the graph paper and thus ON A WARP. Warps that form the edge of a design become the "turning warps" for those colors.

III. *Counting the turned joint*

Differing from the hooked joint in which only those warps crossing the batten are counted and used, *in the turned joint each individual warp is*

19

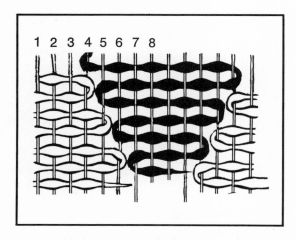

Figure 3.3:
Smooth diagonal in detail.

accounted for. Thus, throughout all turned joint directions, each individual warp will be assigned a number with an L or R following to denote its numerical position to the left or right of center. (TW-33L = your turning warp is the 33rd warp in from the left edge of the weaving.) This is not a Navajo method, and is employed here simply to ease communications.

IV. *Using the turned joint to make a smooth diagonal*

When you are using the turned joint to make a shallow diagonal, your turning warp will be continually changing. Each row will take you one warp further in the direction the design is going. *Do not worry if wefts sometimes turn around adjacent warps rather than the same one. In the next row, the turning warp will move and the overlap will occur* (Fig. 3.3).

V. *Marking the turning warp*

Beginners may find it useful to directly mark the turning warp in use. Just *loosely* tie a piece of string to the current turning warp about 8 inches up from the weaving. In this way you can easily locate the one in use, yet also move the marker as the design progresses. This should be considered a temporary aid.

Rules

There are three rules that may make your learning easier. Read them now; they will become clearer with application.

I. *Which Yarn to Start With*

> *When row is going to the left, start with yarn on left.*
> *When row is going to the right, start with yarn on right.*

20

As you apply this rule you will notice that the last yarn used in one row will be the first to be used in the next row. If you follow this rule, you will avoid one of the pitfalls — accidental hooking. (By beginning the row with the yarn indicated, you clear the path ahead and no hooking can occur.)

II. *When to Circle a "Turning Warp"*

Sometimes the turning warp will be in front of the batten and sometimes in back. The following rule will tell you when to circle it immediately, and when to leave it for the next row:

When turning warp is in back; ignore it.
When turning warp is in front; include it.

III. *When to Move the Marker*

As you are weaving your smooth diagonal, the turning warp will be continually changing. After it has been circled twice (once by each color) you will move the marker one warp in the direction you want your design to go.

Looking at Figure 3.3, notice that warps 4, 5 and 6 are circled twice, first by the white and then by the black. Note, too, that the white side shapes are decreasing while the black is increasing. Thus the rule for the smooth diagonal:

The decreasing shape circles the turning warp first!

In setting up each new smooth diagonal, it is often necessary to move a turning warp that has been circled only once. This happens when the design change causes the *increasing* yarn to circle a turning warp before the *decreasing* yarn can. In this instance, just move your marker right away, giving the decreasing yarn a new turning warp to circle first.

For clarification, please refer to Figure 3.3 again. Here warp 7 was the first turning warp on the left. However, since black (increasing) used it first, the turning warp was circled just once, and then changed to 6. Here, white (decreasing) could circle it first as per the rule and then be followed by black (increasing). Once again, the situation will clarify with doing.

The "Butterfly" design

You will encounter many designs which require a smooth diagonal.* Generally these designs are just elaborations of several basic shapes: decreasing triangles, increasing triangles and parallelograms.

---

*For additional ideas of diagonal designs to render in the turned joint, see the Crystal patterns in Chapter 6 and the Crystal and saddle blankets in Chapter 5. Additionally the "Morning Star" design for the two-faced, Chapter 7, can also be woven in regular weave using the turned joint.

Figure 3.4: *Basic smooth diagonal shapes requiring the turned joint.*

One such interesting pattern is the so-called "Butterfly" design. Based exclusively on diagonals, it provides good experience in the turned joint while offering a challenging experience in interlocking shapes. We have graphed it here for you and have recorded some step-by-step instructions just to get you started. Refer to the chart for warping specifics. Then when you have woven 2¼", begin the instructions for the decreasing triangle pattern.

THE DECREASING TRIANGLE
IN THE "BUTTERFLY" DESIGN

Numbered warps here refer to the first part of the Butterfly design. However, any number can be substituted and the directions followed for decreasing designs of other dimensions.

Row 1: STICK SHED ←

Begin by marking your turning warps: TW-34L and TW-34R. Then:
1. Lay in left yarn behind 17 front warps.
2. Lay in center yarn behind 7 middle warps.
3. Lay in right yarn behind 17 front warps.

Row 2: PULL SHED →

1. Enter shed at 34R (it is in back of the batten; ignore it as per rule II). Move marker 1 warp to L. 35R = new turning warp.*
2. TW-L → TW-R. Enter shed at TW-L. (It's in front of batten. Include by circling around behind it before entering shed.) Come out at 35R. (Include front warp.)
3. Edge → TW-L. Insert yarn at edge and come out at 34L. (Include front warp.)

Row 3: STICK SHED ←

1. Edge ← TW-L. Left TW is in back of batten; ignore and take yarn to L edge. Since TW-L has been circled twice, move marker 1 warp to R. 35L = new TW.

* In setting up this new design, TW-34R is circled just once. Remember the rule, the decreasing design circles the turning warp first.

22

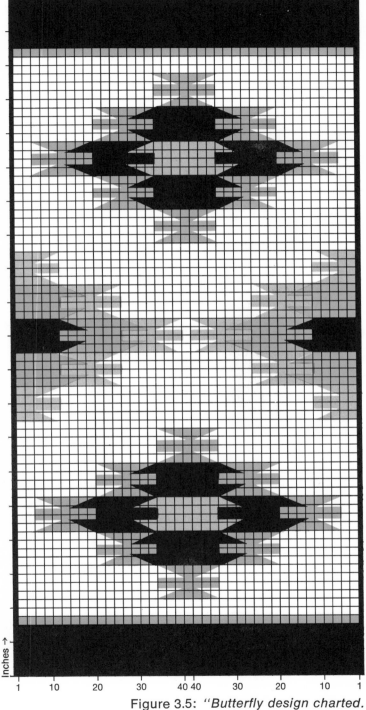

"BUTTERFLY" DESIGN

Size: 10″ x 20″

Weft required: 8½ oz.
- ☐ Light: 4 oz.
- ▨ Medium: ⅔ oz.
- ■ Dark: 2⅓ oz.
- ▨ Bright: 1½ oz.

Warp required: 50 yards

Warping particulars:
    Dowel 1 = 41 marks
    Dowel 2 = 40 marks
Warping frame nails:
    18½″ apart

Inches →

1 10 20 30 40 40 30 20 10 1

Figure 3.5: *"Butterfly design charted.*

2. TW-L ← TW-R. TW-R is in back (ignore). Come out at new TW-L which is a front warp (include).

3. TW-R ← Edge. Enter shed at edge and come out at TW-R — a back warp (ignore).

Row 4: PULL SHED →

1. TW-R → Edge. Enter shed by circling around behind TW-R. Since TW-R has been circled twice, move marker 1 warp to L. (36R = new TW.)

2. TW-L → TW-R. TW-L is in back; ignore it and enter shed. Come out at TW-R (back; ignore).

3. Edge → TW-L. Enter shed. Come out at TW-L (back; ignore).

Row 5: STICK SHED ←

1. Edge ← TW-L. Enter shed at TW-L (front; include). Marker moves 1 warp R. (36L = new TW.)

2. TW-L ← TW-R. Enter shed at TW-R (front; include). Come out at TW-L (back; ignore).

3. TW-R ← Edge. Enter shed. Come out at TW-R (front; include).

Row 6: PULL SHED →

1. TW-R → Edge. Enter shed at TW-R (back; ignore). TW-R has been circled twice. Move marker to 37R.

2. TW-L → TW-R. Enter shed at TW-L (front; include). Come out at TW-R (front; include).

3. Edge → TW-L. Enter shed. Come out at TW-L (front; include).

Continue with the sequence described here, repeating rows 3 through 6 until the design almost peaks. As you build your designs just remember that when you have circled your turning warp twice (once with each color) move it one warp in the direction you want your design to go. Also remember that the slant that you achieve will vary from weaver to weaver. Just work your way upward, watching proportions develop, and feeling free to embellish or simplify here or at the half, to create a symmetrical weaving.

Sectioned weaving
(when width of weaving exceeds your batten)

When a weaving is wider than the batten is long, the Navajo weaver usually weaves the rug in sections. Such an approach allows her to remain in one position for a period of weaving, rather than to reposition her batten and herself several times in each row.

Since this technique is considered to require less effort on the part of the weaver, and also because of the resulting faint line between woven sections, the term "lazy line" has unfortunately become associated with the technique.

I. *The technique*

Sectioned areas are built-up diagonally with the turned joint (each successive row going one individual warp more or less than the last). As an adjoining section is woven, it dovetails and overlaps the previous one, raising the weaving to an even line once more.

II. *The sequence of sectioning is most important*

It is essential that the first section decreases as it rises, thus creating an "open" adjacent area. To do otherwise is to "close-off" the unwoven area and make it inaccessible.

III. *Additional considerations*

Most often weavers time their sections around the pattern, placing the overlap in solid background areas. In these instances the diagonals are not altogether imperceptible in the finished product. Since hand-dyed colors vary within a skein, separately woven adjoining sections emphasize whatever color streaking is present. In addition, when a sectionally woven rug is positioned against light, the line is further accentuated by a diagonal of small light holes.

To avoid these irregularities, simply coordinate design and technique, using the sectional technique for build-up only at the edge of a diagonal pattern where color change is intentional. Some weavers plan their design with sectional build-ups in mind.

In an opposite vein, color variations can be considered beautiful and interesting. To this end sectional weaving may be used and even exploited to create subtle nuances within an otherwise large and uninteresting area.

25

CHAPTER 4

Combine Both Hooked and Turned Joints

HOOKED AND TURNED JOINTS are often combined in the same rug — the hooked being used for verticals, the turned for smooth diagonals. Since the joints have differing techniques, using the two together requires some practice.

The eagle in Figure 4.1* gives good experience in both types. It begins with solely the hooked (verticals in tail), in case you need review or want practice in eliminating ridges. It then changes to just the turned (diagonals in tail), again for practice and review. The next innovation, however, returns the hooked along with the turned, and thus the adventure begins!

Ideas for using this design include weaving eagles in both halves of your project, perhaps each with a different color emphasis. The weaving could then be used flat or folded into a small pillow with eagles of a different color on each side. On the other hand you could design your own bottom half and weave an eagle on the top, with thoughts toward a purse. (A purse with eagles on both sides would require the bottom eagle to be inverted.) A third thought is a wall hanging in which the eagle is centered between stripes of varying widths. Additional pattern or tufting could be added if greater complexity is desired.

To aid you in getting started, general counts for the tail will be given. When the dual joining begins, specific directions will start. As in other patterns, but especially in pictorials, your eagle may be shorter or taller than

* Charting and warping particulars: 4 squares = 1″. Dowel 1 has 41 marks, dowel 2 has 40 marks. Project size 10″ x 20″ (warping frame nails 18½″ apart).

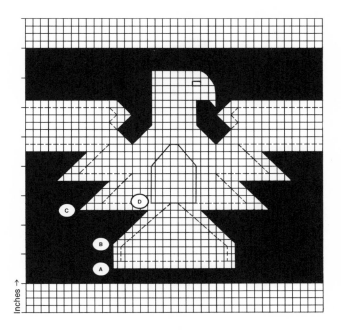

Figure 4.1: *Eagle design charted which combines hooked and turned joints.*

the one drawn here. This is the result of many variables including your warp spacing, size of weft, and amount of packing. Therefore, please be prepared to create space-saving or space-using innovations as the need arises.

Additionally, since this pattern represents both joint types, it will be assumed that some prior experience has been had with each. A review may also be helpful (pp. 64–66 WWW; and Chapter 3 of this book).

Directions for beginning the eagle

If complexity of design is appealing, you may want to outline the eagle as indicated by the dotted lines in the figure. Directions that follow, however, will pertain to the simplified shape without outlining. The following abbreviations will be used: L = left; R = right; CTR = center; BKG = background.

THE TAIL

Begin the tail of your eagle with the hooked joint, using as your count: 12-

16-12. Note that the verticals are drawn between warps to indicate the hooked joint.

When the tail is just past the ¾" mark, change to the turned joint and the decreasing diagonal as follows:

STICK SHED ←: insert yarns just as before.

PULL SHED →: begin turned warp procedure in this order:

1. R-BKG yarn to edge behind 12 front warps.
2. CTR yarn behind 16 front warps.
3. L-BKG yarn behind 12 front warps.

STICK SHED ←

1. L-BKG yarn around 25L (25th individual warp on left side) and to L edge. (It's a front warp; include it!)
2. CTR yarn in at 25R (back warp; ignore). Out at 26L (back; ignore).
3. R-BKG yarn in at edge. Out at 25R (back; ignore).

PULL SHED →

1. L-BKG yarn in at edge; out at 26L (front; include).
2. CTR yarn around 26 L (front; include); out at 26R (back; ignore).
3. R-BKG yarn around 25 R (front; include); out at edge.

Continue weaving, using turned joint technique until your center yarn count is behind 8 front warps, as per figure.

THE WING

Referring to the figure for count, increase your design to begin the left and right wings (C). After approximately ¼" begin the verticals inside the body (D). Directions follow.

STICK SHED ←: Lay in new center yarn behind center 6 front warps. Add left wing yarn.

PULL SHED →: At this point you will be combining hooked and turned joints. The sequence of yarns used will change from row to row. Please think through the next three rows so that when directions stop *you* will be able to continue.

Refer to Figure 16 for sequence of yarns in this row.

1. R-BKG yarn to edge.
2. L-wing decreases design and goes to CTR yarn. Hook!
3. CTR yarn goes behind 6 front warps to R-wing. Hook!
4. R-wing yarn goes to R-BKG yarn.
5. L-BKG increases design.

28

Figure 4.2: *Yarn order for combined hooked and turned joints in eagle.*

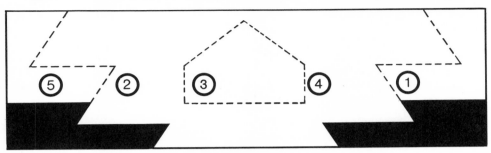

| 5. L-BKG increases design. | 2. L-wing decreases design and goes to CTR yarn. HOOK! | 3. CTR yarn goes behind 6 front warps to R-wing. HOOK! | 4. R-wing yarn goes to R-BKG yarn. | 1. R-BKG yarn to edge. |

PULL SHED → RULES FOR COMBINED HOOKED AND TURNED JOINTS

Start with yarn on right and work progressively left as in the turned joint technique.

If the joint is a turned joint — do it!

IF NOT: Continue checking each yarn to the left until you find the next turned joint yarn.

Do it and complete the hooking sequence that will follow! Continue this procedure for the row.

Reflect on the past row and on the above rules. Take the row out and reweave if necessary to help you understand the principles involved. When you feel secure as to procedure, continue with directions, applying these lessons in each pull shed.

STICK SHED ←: Use sequential order — left to right — as in regular turned joint technique.

1. L-BKG to L edge.
2. L-wing to L-BKG (decrease design).
3. CTR yarn behind 6 front warps to L-wing.
4. R-wing to CTR.
5. R-BKG to R-wing (increase design).

PULL SHED →: *This is your last row with directions. Review pull-shed rules above if necessary.*

1. R-BKG to R edge.
2. L-wing to CTR yarn. HOOK!
3. CTR yarn behind 6 front warps to R-wing. HOOK!
4. R-wing to R-BKG.
5. L-BKG to L edge.

Continue your weaving using the approach you have learned so far. Feel free to elaborate or simplify as situations occur. Stand back from your weaving frequently to see the overall shape and progress.

Working with two joints simultaneously can be an exhilarating experience — success in the face of complexity! If this is your concluding feeling, your next project might be a larger one combining these two joints. One such has been charted for you in Chapter 5 — "The Storm Pattern." Or you may prefer to design your own, referring to Chapter 8 for charting ideas. Regardless of what's ahead, you can take pride in the pinnacle of skill you have achieved here.

CHAPTER 5

Think Big!

ENCOURAGED BY THE SUCCESS of several smaller projects, your thoughts may be turning to something bigger. *A real rug* you say! Something to *walk* on? A *large* tapestry for the wall? If these are your aspirations, this chapter with its designs and directions was written for you!

The project: what size?

Many aspects of the project depend on the size you select. Here are considerations to help with your decision.

20″ x 40″?

This size rug takes advantage of the 10″ x 20″ designs drawn throughout this book. They can easily be enlarged to twice the width and length. A rug 20″ x 40″ can be woven on your *Working with the Wool* loom if you convert it to accept warp that is longer than the loom is high. Described as the "Up-and-Over" technique, it receives full directions within the chapter.

30″ x 30″?

A popular size for horse lovers, this single saddle blanket dimension can also be woven on your 3′ x 4′ loom. Because the length is not unwieldy, you do not need to use the "Up-and-Over" technique. Simply change bottom and top dowel-beams to ¾″ pipes, refastening the latter with pipe straps as high up as possible on the loom.

Tufting (Chapter 6) is a quickly vanishing technique, but makes a lovely saddle blanket, with long mohair locks gently framing the saddle. Another saddle blanket design is drawn here with an ornate border and simple center, again appropriate to being used beneath the saddle. The inversion technique for finishing such patterns is recommended and described.

30″ x 48″?

This size takes advantage of the design drawn in the back of *Working with the Wool,* p. 99. It, too, can be woven on your converted 3′ x 4′ loom, or a larger loom can be built. If using the converted loom drill additional side holes to meet your needs.

30″ x 60″?

The two-faced diamond twill (Chapter 7) or the single saddle blanket design can be adjusted to yield this double saddle blanket size and woven either on the converted loom or on a larger one. If the converted loom is used, once again drill additional side holes to meet your needs.

3′ x 5′? 4′ x 6′? 5′ x 7′?

Now you're in the *big* leagues and your loom should match. Ideas for larger looms and designs follow the "Up-and-Over" section.

The "up-and-over" technique

When weaving a rug with dimensions greater than the height of the loom, the "up-and-over" technique can be employed with good results. This method ties the bottom of the warp to the bottom loom beam as usual. The rest of the warp, however, goes up and over the top beam and is then roped and tightened *behind* the weaving. As your work progresses beyond arm reach, your weaving is rolled under and away to unfurl new warp at the top.

Directions here will specifically refer to converting the WWW loom.

LOOM MODIFICATION

I. *Materials needed:*

One ½″ black pipe,* length of loom width
Two ¾″ black pipes, length of loom width
Wire: as heavy as possible but still pliable

II. *Directions for loom modification:*
(Please refer to Figure 5.1 throughout.)

*Fraction measurements refer to pipe's *inside* diameter.

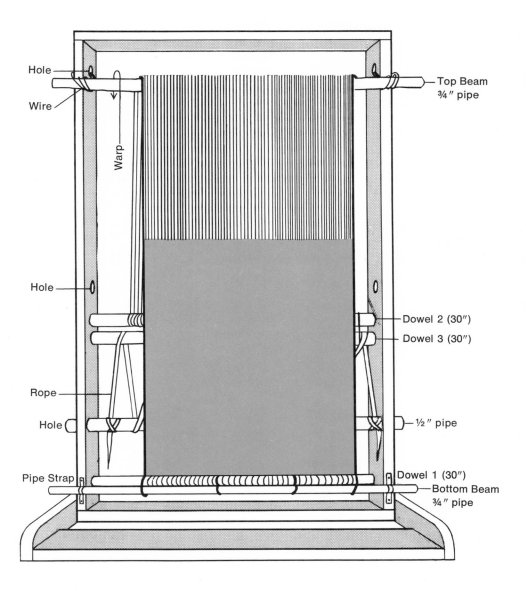

Hole

Wire

Warp

Hole

Rope

Hole

Pipe Strap

Top Beam
¾" pipe

Dowel 2 (30")

Dowel 3 (30")

½" pipe

Dowel 1 (30")
Bottom Beam
¾" pipe

Figure 5.1: *A long warp mounted up and over top beam of converted loom.*

1. *Remove all dowels* from loom.
2. *Position bottom beam* by inserting one ¾" pipe in bottom pipe straps.
3. *Drill three ⅞" holes* in both vertical posts of loom at 12", 24", and 40" measured from floor. These holes accommodate a variety of project sizes. However, if in your warp-rolling you find you need additional holes, feel free to drill them.
4. *Position top beam* by wiring second ¾" pipe using top hole made in step 3 above.
5. *Insert ½" pipe* into bottom hole made in step 3. This will receive your rope on the back side of the loom and be described more fully later.

DIRECTIONS FOR WARPING

Since your three warping dowels will be positioned inside the loom frame as you roll your warp, they should be less than the inside loom dimension. For wider weavings and longer dowels, see "Additional Considerations" below.

DIRECTIONS FOR MOUNTING WARP ON LOOM
(Please refer to Figure 5.1 throughout.)

1. Wire bottom warped dowel (no. 1 with knots) flush with bottom pipe at 7" intervals. Turn sharp wire ends out of the way.
2. Direct dowel no. 2 over top pipe and let it hang inside loom frame.
3. Wire dowels no. 2 and 3 together, 1" apart and at 7" intervals. Turn sharp wire ends out of the way.
4. The final step, that of attaching and tightening the rope, depends on your warp length. Standing behind the loom, position the ½" pipe that will receive the rope in whatever hole is closest to dowel no. 3 — but allows at least 5" space between the two. Then encircle dowel no. 3 and the ½" pipe, using the "over-and-away; under-and-toward," left-to-right direction as usual. Cinch to tighten, progressing right to left (p. 38 WWW). Muscle up and bear down! *You will be tired before it's tight!*

DIRECTIONS FOR ROLLING RUG UNDER AS WEAVING PROGRESSES

Timing and distances here will vary depending on warp length. For use as a guide, the following directions will apply to a 20" x 40" warp:
1. When approximately 20" has been woven in original position, release weaving by removing rope from back and wire from bottom pipe.
2. Direct bottom of weaving beneath bottom pipe. Wire it to the ½" pipe moved to center hole.
3. Attach rope to top beam and dowel no. 3 as per regular method.

ADDITIONAL CONSIDERATIONS

1. The "up-and-over" technique is not recommended for beginners.

2. The method described above houses rope arrangement inside the loom frame, thus *freeing the back of the loom for a small additional weaving* (i.e. 10″ x 23″).

3. By securing the rope arrangement to the back side of the loom, instead of within, the 30″ x 48″, 30″ x 30″, or 30″ x 60″ projects can be accommodated. In these instances, warping dowel length should exceed the loom width. These dowels, held in back of the loom, can be *wired* to the same holes.

Building your large loom

When building your large loom simply follow the same principles used in making your WWW loom (p. 8 WWW).

1. Construct your loom of large timbers, being certain it is sturdy!

2. Plan to house the weaving in front of the loom proper so batten will not be hindered by vertical posts. Top and bottom beams that are longer than width of loom will hold warp in the desired forward position.

Because this is a larger loom, some additional considerations come into play:

1. *Large looms require much effort when tightening the warp.* When Tiana Bighorse's mother wove large rugs, her husband would hitch up his team of horses to provide the necessary tightening power. Some more modern weavers (such as those at Hubbell's Trading Post in Ganado, Arizona) have exchanged the rope for turnbuckles. They are tied at 12″ intervals between top beam and dowel no. 3. Tightening the warp is then easily accomplished by turning all buckles evenly.

2. *A large loom makes a lovely room divider.* Care must be taken though that light does not stream through the warp into the weaver's eyes. If necessary, a dark cloth can be hung behind the warps to block light while the loom is in use.

3. *There are many different styles of looms.* If you are going to use lumber, consider 2″ x 6″, 2″ x 8″, or even 2″ x 12″ side posts. The wider the sides, the larger the holes can be drilled if the up-and-over technique is used. For some illustrations of large lumber looms, see these sources:

Arizona Highways, July 1974 — p. 16, note warp held in front of frame; p. 38, note that the warp is housed inside the frame, but that the sides had to be recessed to allow for batten action.

Arizona Highways, July 1976 — p. 15, note turnbuckles instead of rope for tensioner; cover, note sturdy loom of welded metal.

4. *Log looms are a lovely alternative to lumber-built looms.* Traditionally styled and more natural in appearance, these looms are unfortunately more difficult to build. Traditionally, upright logs were once part of the hogan, or simply trees that grew the right distance apart. In these instances, anchoring for loom use was no problem. In our more modern times of cement-based floors, etc., other methods need to be used. One idea is to drill ¼" holes (cement bit) spaced for loom width into the cement-based floor and again into post bottoms. A ¼" metal spike is then driven into floor holes and the posts placed on top. A firm floor attachment is then achieved. Ceiling attachments vary with conditions. One idea is to insert eye screws (3" shaft, ½" eye) through the ceiling material and into ceiling supports. A ½" bolt can then be inserted through the eye and the log posts.

As for fastening top and bottom beams to these anchored posts, small holes can be drilled at desired height to receive the wire that will firmly hold beams in place.

To give you other ideas on authentic construction, you can consult Arizona Highways's *Arizona's Colorful Indians,* 1967. There are two illustrations that feature log looms, the last of which uses especially lovely posts of notable size!

Warping your large loom

When warping your large loom, refer to page 25 WWW which shows the weaver seated *inside the frame.* If the warp will be huge, you may need help. One weaver north of Tuba City, Arizona, positions herself in the center of her 8' x 12' frame. One daughter is then given the ball of warp to carry and encircles the first dowel. She returns it to her mother who applys the proper tension. At this point daughter number two is given the warp-ball to repeat the process on the second dowel. And so it goes across the frame.

Since warp tension is so critical and larger warpings tend to compound tension problems, please refer to Chapter 1 and the proper correction of warp once it is mounted on the loom.

A second warping consideration is spacing. If the rug is to receive heavy floor use, you might consider spacing your warps 6 per inch (three marks per inch on each dowel) for a heavier product and faster weaving. Your weft should then be appropriately larger so that the warp/weft relationship will be right. Once again, Chapter 1 treats the subject more fully.

Weaving on your large loom

One of the problems encountered in weaving on your larger rug will be that the width of your weaving is more than the batten length. Resist getting a

SINGLE SADDLE BLANKET

Size: 30″ x 30″

Weft required: 2½ lbs.
☐ White: 1½ lb.
■ Black: ½ lb.
▨ Color: ½ lb.
(red or ochre)

*Warp required: 500 yards
*Warping particulars:
Dowel 1 = 121 marks
Dowel 2 = 120 marks
Warping frame nails:
28½″ apart

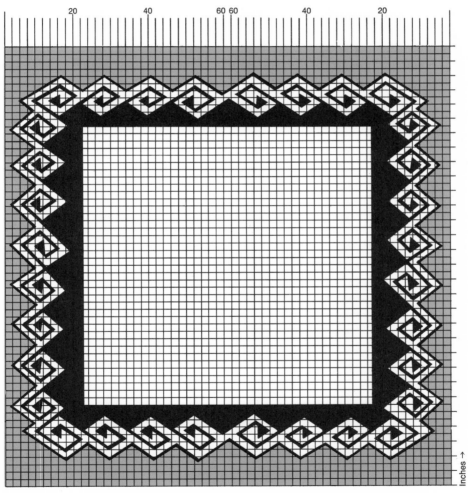

Figure 5.2: *Single saddle blanket design charted.*

long, unwieldy batten, for it will tire you to the point of incompletion. The Navajo method is a technique which can be referred to as "sectioned weaving," in which areas are woven diagonally — each adjoining section overlapping a previous one and raising the weaving to an even line once again. Using as it does the turned joint, the technique is further described in Chapter 3 of this book.

Designing for your large loom

We have drawn several designs here to help you formulate ideas:

The first is a 30" x 30" saddle blanket with an ornate border to frame the saddle. Since the center is plain, most weavers finish the weaving in the middle using the "inversion technique." Description of this finishing method follows the charting.

The second design is the so-called "Chief Blanket." Based on vertical lines, it can be woven in hooked joints exclusively (Chapter 2). This particular design was a favorite to wear, as half diamonds along the edges come together in front of the wearer creating a dramatic and lovely covering. Some weavers today simply consider the design one that indicates their skill as a weaver; each side folded in should not only match the center diamond, but align with each other.

The two Crystal designs, on the other hand, use only the turned joint (Chapter 3) and are suggested in lovely plant hues. Since the rugs are positioned vertically on the loom, the Corn Crystal design will be woven sideways.

As a final consideration, you might give thought to the "Storm Pattern" which is charted to combine both hooked and turned joints. Colors are optional, of course, but the traditional black, white, grey and red have been noted for consideration. The "Storm Pattern" is a satisfying design to work with, being one of the few rug patterns with meaning attached. As usual, stories vary from weaver to weaver, but one of the most common descriptions is that this is a pattern for rain. In the center is water-potential which the weaver hopes will spread and envelop the entire reservation: thus the four rectangles at the four corners — to indicate the four sacred mountains which bound the reservation, or the four directions. "May there be enough for all."

An additional hope is that the rain be the soft, gentle female-type that urges the plants to grow (thus the misnomer "Storm Pattern"). The fruits of its nurturing power are indicated on top and bottom: first a symbol of animal life (water bug) and then one for plant life.

If you would rather design your own rug, you might refer to Chapter 8

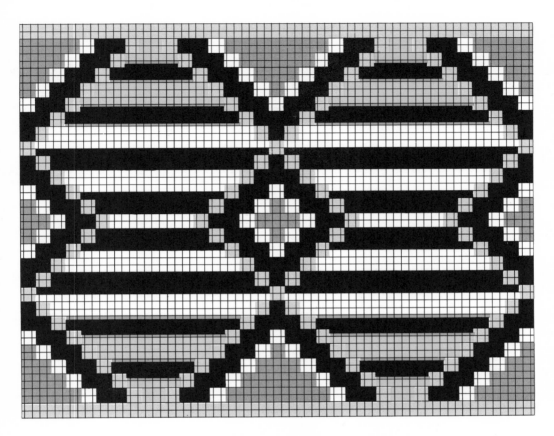

Figure 5.3: *Chief Blanket design charted.*

Weft amount:
- ■ Black: 2 lb.
- □ White: 1 lb.
- ▨ Red: 1 lb.
- ▨ Grey: 8 oz.
- ▨ Blue: 6 oz.
- ▨ Orange: 2 oz. (for very thin stripes only)

Size: 3′ x 3′9″

*Warp amount: 360 yards

*Warping particulars:
   Dowel 1 = 181 marks
   Dowel 2 = 180 marks
Warping frame nails:
   2′10½″ apart

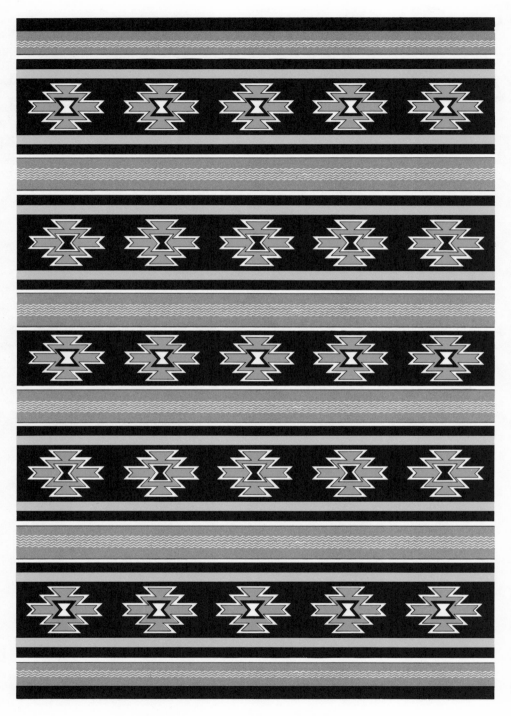

Figure 5.4: *Traditional Crystal design.*

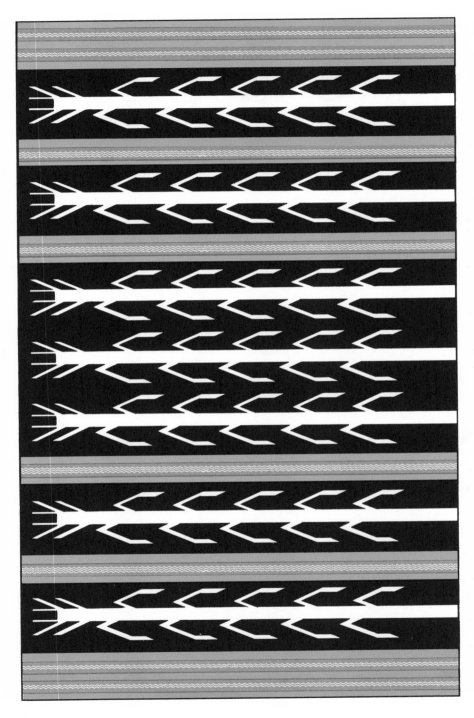

Figure 5.5: *Corn Crystal design.*

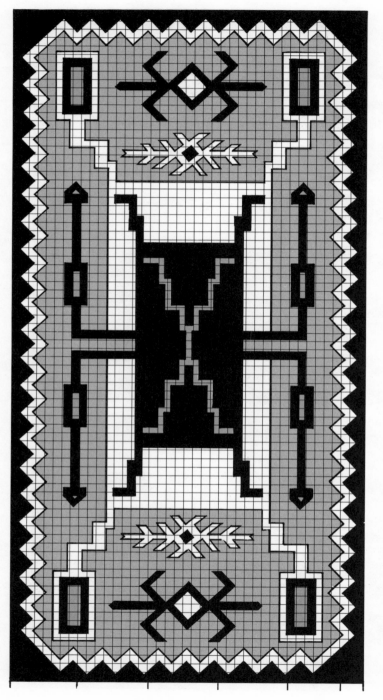

Figure 5.6: *Storm Pattern design charted.*

for ideas on charting and computing warp and weft. Another helpful section may be the book list in the back pages, which will direct you to many other design ideas.

The inversion technique
(for finishing ornately bordered rugs)

Most Navajo rugs are designed with solid stripes at the beginning and end of the rug so as to simplify the final and tedious two inches.

An alternative to finishing a weaving at the top, is that of completing it in the center. This is especially appropriate when the design has a solid center as in saddle blankets with ornate borders (Fig. 5.2). To finish by this method:

1. First weave upward from the bottom to the beginning of the solid center section.

2. Then remove dowels no. 1 and 2 from the loom and invert the project, being certain to first tie willow sticks together! Remount and retighten.

3. Adjust the shed/heddle arrangement by removing willow shed rod from below heddles and reinserting it above them. (This can easily be done by inserting your batten next to the stick in its lower position. Turn it on edge. Remove stick and replace in opening above heddles.)

You are now ready to begin weaving. First enter your four rows to correspond to the usual first four rows of weaving (over and under pairs). Continue weaving using regular sheds as before and your finishing will be centralized.

CHAPTER 6

Be Adventurous —
Sample Them All!

IN THE TRADITIONAL WAY, Navajo weavers begin with striped rugs and ease slowly into more complex designs. Somewhere in their course, they may be fortunate enough to be shown the "Coal Mine" or even the diamond twill. At this time they simply warp a new rug, and weave it through in that technique. The pride in acquisition of knowledge is considerable and many Navajo weavers equate their mastery of the craft with how many types of weaves they know.

Today there are students of the craft that find it preferable to sample techniques before committing the time to a full rug. For these people, a project has been designed which combines eight advanced techniques into a pleasing whole:

Tufting
Turned Joint (doubled-cross motif)
Coal Mine Raised Edge
Small Diamond Twill
Pictorial
Medium Diamond Twill
Two-Faced
Crystal

WARPING

Sampler size: 10″ x 23″
41 marks on dowel no. 1; 40 marks on dowel no. 2.
Warping nails 20½″ apart.

45

YARN

Though any combination of colors may be used, the directions refer to four: black, white, brown, and grey (3 oz. each of the first three, 1 oz. of the last). If you choose your own colors, pick four distinct shades — clarity is especially important while you learn the Coal Mine and diamond twill.

WEAVING

As you change from one technique to another in the same weaving, skills will be strongly tested. Some techniques will not allow you to fill in; an even weaving line will be achieved only by maintaining well-distributed warps. Some techniques will require different amounts of weft; your scallop size will have to be adjusted appropriately so that edges will be straight.

CHART

The weaving has been photographed so you can visualize the overall effect beforehand. There is also a descriptive chart. It refers to each section in the sampler indicating the purpose, size and possible colors. Since the designs appear here in the same sequence as in the woven sampler, please read the chart from the bottom up — just like you are weaving. Full directions for each technique will be given in separate sections.

Tufting

Tufting is an old Navajo technique using long goat or sheep hair to give a fleece effect.

Some of the older Navajo women, reminiscing about ages past, speak of sleeping on the packed dirt floor of the hogan. Sheepskins would be brought forth for the night — some placed directly on the ground to lay upon, and some reserved as a cover.

Design	Inches*	Colors	Additional Comments
Plain Weave	1½ "	Black	The simplest design — positioned last to promote a *finished* weaving!
Tufting	1"	White	Tufting at top may be positioned as indicated in sampler, if weaving is to be used flat. When weaving is hung, however, some weavers prefer to expand the Crystal section (to 1½") reducing plain weave proportionately. When tufting hangs down, Crystal will not be obscured.
Doubled-Cross Motif	1"	Brown White	See initial description.
Crystal	1"	Black Brown Grey White	A simple technique, characterized by horizontal wavy lines and positioned near the top to make the finishing flow!
Two-Faced Doubled-Cross Motif	1"	Black Brown Grey White	Doubled-cross motif on the front in black and white variegated stripes on the back (in grey and brown)!
Medium Diamond Twill	3½ "	Black Brown White	Larger concentric diamonds and a different color emphasis on each side of the fabric. Section on interesting variations included.
Pictorial	4"	Black White Brown	Pictorial (plus variation on doubled-cross motif) provides central design of sampler and additional practice in the turned joint.
Small Diamond Twill	3½ "	Black Brown White	Small diamonds stacked upon each other. Different color emphasis on each side of weaving. Fun to improvise!
Doubled-Cross Motif	1"	White Black	See description below.
Coal Mine Raised Edge	2"	Black Brown Grey White	Design outlined by a raised edge with small vertical pinstripes permeating.
Doubled-Cross Motif	1"	Brown White	A repetitive motif that unifies sampler and provides exposure to the turned joint.
Tufting	1"	White	An old Navajo technique using long goat or sheep hair to give a fleece look. Broken yarns may be substituted.
Plain Weave	1½ "	Black	For beginning (and ending) ease!

*These are approximate.

Feel free to enlarge segments of any section which captures your interest. Or you may reduce a section when you are satisfied that you have mastered the technique involved.

Proper tanning of hides was a long and complicated process. When done in a hurry (as most were), the result was a rough, inflexible hide. In response to these aspects, the technique of tufting developed — a softly woven article with long goat tufts incorporated. Not only was it flexible enough to curl about the sleeper and close off air holes, but in addition it could be made of any size.

Since beds have largely replaced sleeping on the ground, tufting is only infrequently seen today.

I. *The tufted project*

Tufting is most often used exclusively in a large weaving such as a soft rug or saddle blanket. Here, however, directions will refer to two 1" stripes within the 10" x 23" sampler.

II. *Materials needed*

Goat tufts: *Gently* swish long goat or sheep hair first in soapy, then in rinse water. Let dry. Then pull off the "wisps" or curls of hair that hang together. You will need 52 tufts for each stripe.

Substitute: If fleece is unavailable, you can use 4"–6" pieces of weft, instead. Since *two together will replace each tuft,* you will need 104 individual pieces for each stripe. When using yarn, be certain to break the pieces so ends will be soft and wispy (p. 53 WWW).

Yarn: Wind some yarn that matches the goat tufts onto a stick-shuttle (p. 52 WWW).

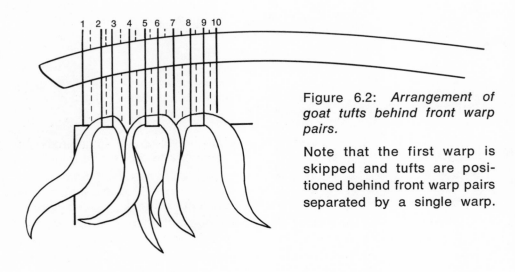

Figure 6.2: *Arrangement of goat tufts behind front warp pairs.*

Note that the first warp is skipped and tufts are positioned behind front warp pairs separated by a single warp.

III. *Specific weaving instructions*
Second stripe on sampler

1. Gather together 13 tufts.
2. Insert batten in stick-shed.
3. Terminate any existing yarn. (Break off 1″ from right edge and insert in shed.)
4. *Left to right: count only warps in front of batten.* Lay one tuft (or yarn pair) behind warps 2 and 3. Lay a second tuft behind warps 5 and 6. Lay a third one behind warps 8 and 9. Position each tuft so ends hang down evenly and continue with row.

Note that first warp is skipped and tufts are positioned behind front warp pairs separated by a single warp (see Figure 6.2).

5. *Right to left:* Lay yarn (wound on stick-shuttle) in same shed and on top of tufting. Beat in place.
6. *Change shed and direction.* Continue regular weave for over ¼″ to compensate for future packing. Fill in low spots as needed (p. 84 WWW). End with yarn on left.
7. Gather together 13 more tufts. Insert batten in *pull shed* →. Lay in tufts just as before, but note that the shed for the tufting has changed. Throughout the technique tufting will be laid on alternate sheds to distribute warp take-up. When tufting is complete, once again lay yarn right on top of tufts and then continue weaving for another ¼″, ending with yarn on right.
8. Repeat process so tufting stripe is just over 1″ to compensate for future packing.
9. When stripe is complete you may want to pin a cloth over the tufting to prevent other yarns from tangling in it as your sampler continues its course.

The doubled-cross motif
(using the turned joint)

The doubled-cross motif is a unifying theme which repeats at intervals throughout the sampler. Though it is used specifically to provide experience in the turned joint, it is also helpful after the Coal Mine or twills as it allows a weaver to fill in and thus reestablish an even weaving line.

49

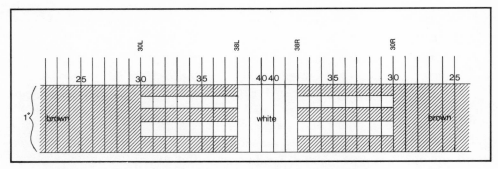

Figure 6.3: *Charting of doubled-cross motif showing yarn order and turning warps 30L, 38L, and 30R.*

For general understanding of the turned joint technique, please refer to Chapter 3, reading sections on General Concept and Rules. Then return here for specific weaving directions.

I. *Specific weaving instructions:*

In the following directions, each individual warp will be numbered and L and R used to indicate the left and right sides of the weaving. Your first turning warps will then be TW-38L (the 38th warp on left of weaving) and TW-38R (the 38th warp on right of weaving). See Figure 6.3. Your second set of turning warps will be 30L and 30R. These two sets alternate throughout the design and can be marked if desired (p. 20).

As you begin weaving, keep the rules of the turned joint well in mind and refer to Figure 6.4 for the way the joints will appear. Then begin row one.

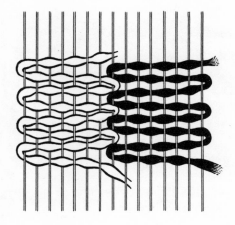

Figure 6.4: *Detail of turned joint, vertical edge.*

50

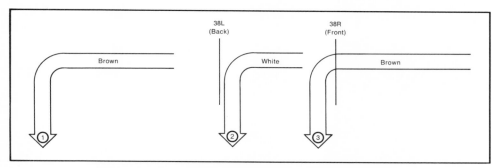

Figure 6.5: *First row of doubled-cross motif
showing yarn order and turning warps.*

Row 1: STICK SHED ←
Begin with yarn on left as numbers indicate (Fig. 6.5).

    1. Lay in brown yarn from 38R to left edge.

    2. Lay in white yarn between 38L and 38R.

    3. Lay in brown yarn from right edge to 38R. It's a front warp, so include it by coming out to its left.

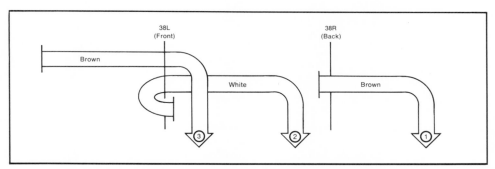

Figure 6.6: *Second row of doubled-cross motif
showing yarn order and turning warps.*

Row 2: PULL SHED →
Begin with yarn on right as numbers indicate (Fig. 6.6).

    1. Cross in front of 38R. (When turning warp is in back of batten, ignore it. Go to right edge.)

    2. Circle around behind 38L. (When turning warp is in front of batten, include it.) Come out to left of 38R. (Turning warp is in back; ignore it.)

    3. Enter shed and come out from behind 38L. (When turning warp is in front of batten, include it.)

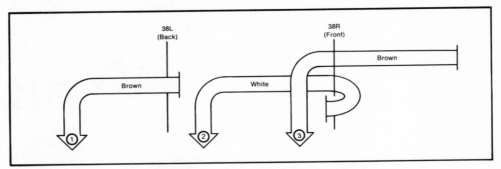

Figure 6.7: *Third row of doubled-cross motif showing yarn order and turning warps.*

Row 3: STICK SHED ←
Begin with yarn on left according to numbers (Fig. 6.7).

    1. Brown yarn crosses in front of 38L (back warp; ignore).

    2. White circles around behind 38R (front; include). Does not include 38L (back; ignore).

    3. Brown includes 38R (front warp).

Row 4 and onward:

    Repeat row 2. Then if design is near ¼ ", stop. If not, rows 3 and 2 can be repeated. Since this is the first of five sections, each section can be almost ¼ ". Then successive packing will reduce the whole to approximately 1".

    With yarn hanging at right of their areas, it is time to change turning warps to 30L and 30R. The diagram below shows the change.

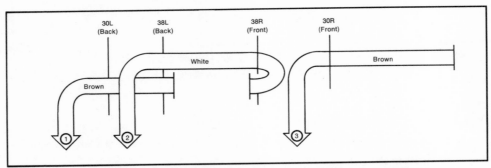

Figure 6.8: *Changing to new count in doubled-cross motif.*

STICK SHED ← *(Row one — new count)*

    1. Brown crosses in front of both and goes to edge (both in back; ignore).

52

2. White circles around behind 38R (front; include) and comes out short of 30L (back; ignore).

3. Brown goes through shed including 30R in its journey. (It's a front warp.)

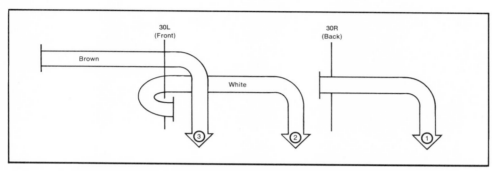

Figure 6.9: *Second row of new count in doubled-cross motif.*

PULL SHED → *(Row 2 — new count)*

1. Brown ignores 30R.
2. White includes 30L but not 30R.
3. Brown includes 30L.

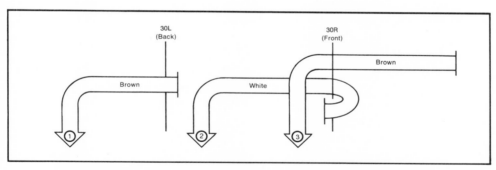

Figure 6.10: *Third row of new count in doubled-cross motif.*

STICK SHED ← *(Row 3 — new count)*

1. Brown ignores 30L.
2. White includes 30R but not 30L.
3. Brown includes 30R.

Once again, repeat row 2 and stop if design is near ¼". If not, repeat rows 3 and 2 again, changing your design back to the original count when your yarns are at the right side. Continue on your own.

II. *Completion*

When doubled-cross is completed, break off yarn ends and insert them into shed as usual. Utilize the finishing rows to fill in and redistribute warps evenly to provide a good base for the Coal Mine to follow.

Coal Mine Raised Edge

The Coal Mine pattern derives its name from its development around Coal Mine Mesa on the western edge of the Navajo Reservation in the 1950s. The characteristic look — that of overall vertical pinstripes — is accomplished by alternating two weft colors through the sheds. When design is incorporated into this technique, separate weft pairs are required for each design area. Where designs meet, weft pairs are manipulated to create a raised outline on the front side of the weave — thus the descriptive title.

I. *The project*

Though directions given here are for a two-inch stripe within the 10″ x 23″ sampler, the Coal Mine Raised Edge technique may be used exclusively in one weaving. In this instance, a beginner would do well to design the project with intermittant solid stripes in which all fill-ins would occur. Likewise in the sampler, the Coal Mine technique should not be started until an even weaving line is established.

A note of emphasis is in order here. Throughout the weaving, it is important to lay weft in especially loosely and maintain sufficient scallops so weft will pack well and cover warp completely without edges drifting inward!

II. *Colors*

The Coal Mine in the sampler will be described in the following colors:
Background: black (leader) and grey (follower)
Design: brown (leader) and white (follower)

III. *Ten general weaving rules for Coal Mine technique*

Please read through these rules before beginning your Coal Mine, being aware that a more complete understanding will follow upon application.

54

1. Turned joint: The Coal Mine is basically a turned-joint technique. As in the turned joint, designs are based on the "smooth diamond" (rather than verticals or steep diagonals). Additionally, there is no hooking of yarns between designs. As a final reminder: *when a row is going to the left, start with the yarn on the left. When the row is going right, start with the yarn on the right* — just like the turned joint.

2. Warp spacing: The Coal Mine Raised Edge technique poses problems in maintaining an even weaving line, as fill-ins of "valleys" are not possible. To minimize difficulty, select uniform yarn for the technique. Also, pay close attention to warp spacing. Remember that when warps ease together in any area, a "hill" will result. Conversely, "valleys" occur in areas where warps have separated. Review technique for warp redistribution (p. 85 WWW) and keep spacing even from the beginning.

3. Leader/Follower concept: It takes two yarns (wefts) — a "leader" and a "follower" — to make each shape.

4. Leader/Follower sheds: The "leader" will always start first in the stick shed. The "follower" will tag along in the same direction, using the pull shed. Thus, *there will always be two rows woven in the same direction.* First two to the left, then two to the right, repeating throughout the weaving.

5. Color choice: When selecting colors, choose closely related ones for the "leader" and "follower" of each shape so the two feel like they belong to each other. In addition, the leaders should relate to each other, and the followers to each other.

(Example: In our particular design, color pairs are black and grey, brown and white. In this set-up the darker of each pair is the leader: black leads grey; brown leads white.)

6. Counting the warps: When deciding how many warps a yarn should include, the term "front warp" will be used to mean just the warps held forward by the batten. When the term "individual warp" is used, this means counting each separate warp at the weaving line. As in the turned joint, L and R indicate warps on left or right half of weaving.

7. Diagonal technique: The diagonal line of a Coal Mine design is made by weaving the leader and then the follower one individual warp further in the direction of increase.

8. Leaders and followers together: Leader and follower yarns often hang out of the weaving together.

a. When a leader and its *own* follower are together, a close look will reveal *an individual warp separating them.* In this instance, *the leader will lead off by crossing beneath the follower* as it starts its row.

b. When a leader and its neighbor's follower are together, close inspection reveals they come out of the *exact same space.* In this instance, it is important to *uncross the two yarns* so they lie next to their own design areas. This happens before a follower begins its row and prevents accidental hooking of wefts.

9. Circling the edge warp: When a yarn is at the side of a weaving and ready to begin a row, make a special effort to circle the edge warp before inserting the yarn into the shed. To do this, disregard whether the edge warp is in front or behind the batten. Just be sure you circle it before inserting the yarn in the shed. (Sometimes two edge warps must be circled together.) This special treatment results in larger-than-usual loops at the selvage.

10. Raised edge effect: Essentially the same procedure occurs when yarns are at the edge of a design. When done correctly, each yarn will begin its trip with a larger-than-usual stitch to circle the first warp. This series of stitches formed at the edge of a design results in the raised edge effect.

IV. *Specific weaving instructions*

Discontinue the three colors remaining from the doubled cross by breaking them off about an inch from the weaving and inserting them into the stick shed. Then wind black and grey yarn onto two shuttles. The directions below are for your first ¼" (refer to sampler drawing). Follow each row for color, direction and technique details.

A. Initial Coal Mine stripe

1. STICK SHED ←: Leader
Lay in background leader (black) for full row.
2. PULL SHED ←: Follower
Lay in background follower (grey) for full row, same direction as leader above (rule 4).
3. STICK SHED →: Background leader (black) for full row. Remember:
a. Leader is always in stick shed (rule 4).
b. At selvage, leader crosses under (in front of) the follower (rule 8a).
c. Before going into shed, leader goes in front of left edge warp so it will be circled (rule 9).
4. PULL SHED →: Background follower (grey), full row. Remember:
a. Follower goes same direction as leader but in pull shed (rule 4).
b. Beginning its row, follower goes in back of left edge warp, so warp will be circled.

By now you should be able to discern small vertical black and grey pinstripes developing within the Coal Mine area. You have also used half the rules given on the previous pages. Reread them for better understanding and continue until your Coal Mine stripe is ¼" and yarns are at right of weaving.

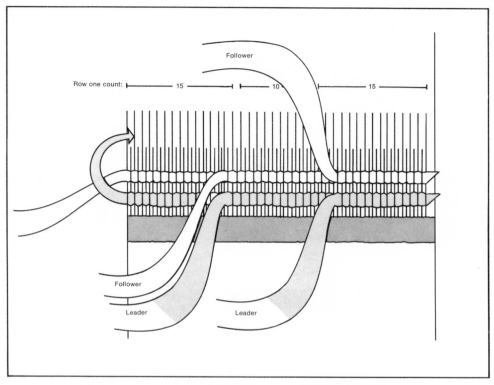

Figure 6.11: *First two rows of Coal Mine design.*

B. Coal Mine design: Increase for 1″

The directions below begin your Coal Mine design with the raised edge. Follow each row thoughtfully, as your design takes shape, referring back to rule section as clarification is needed.

Row 1: STICK SHED ←: Leaders (see Figure 6.11)

There will be three color areas: left background; center design; right background.

Lay in three leader yarns counting *front* warps as follows: black 15; brown 10; black 15 (this yarn continues from the initial ¼″ just woven).

Row 2: PULL SHED ←: Followers (see Figure 6.11)

Lay in three follower yarns in same direction.

Front warp count: grey 14; white 11; grey 15 (this yarn also continues from previous ¼″ weaving).

The count change here indicates the background areas are decreasing one individual warp while the design is increasing.

Row 3: STICK SHED →: Leaders only

Situation: yarn pairs hanging at left of design areas.

Refer to rules 6, 7, 8 and 10 as needed.

Since row is going to the right, begin with leader on right.

1. Right black yarn (right leader) enters row by crossing beneath and to the right of the grey. It enters shed just left of the 14th front warp on the right of the weaving and comes out at the edge.

2. Brown yarn (center leader) is inserted to right of front warp 16L. It then continues behind the next 10 front warps, coming out in the same space as the grey yarn (right background follower). Counting individual warps, this space would be between 29R and 30R. Look closely at this yarn's trip. It goes over 2 individual warps on the left before going into shed. This creates the extra-long stitch that is responsible for the raised-edge technique.

3. Left black yarn (left background leader) crosses to right beneath the grey, circles in front of first warp and enters shed for next 14 front warps. This will bring it out into the same space as the white yarn (center follower). Once again counting individual warps, this space occurs between 29L and 30L.

This row is of particular importance in understanding several rules. It well demonstrates the "crossing-under" that occurs when a leader and its follower are at the design edge. Additionally, it repeats the raised outline stitches that occur at a design edge. And finally, the leaders are coming out *in the exact same space* as their neighboring followers. As you put batten in next shed, you will need to *uncross* these two yarns so they lie next to their own design area (rule 8b).

Row 4: PULL SHED →: Followers only (uncross yarn pairs).
(Row goes to right; begin with yarn on right)

1. Right grey (follower) enters shed behind 14 front warps and goes to right edge.

2. White yarn (center follower) enters shed behind front warp 16L. It comes out after 11 front warps, *which is one individual warp more than its leader.*

3. Left grey (follower) circles behind edge warp and into shed for 14 front warps. It comes out *1 individual warp short of its leader.*

Please note that in this row, each design yarn started its trip 1 individual warp more or less than its own leader.

Row 5: STICK SHED ←: Leaders only

Situation: All yarns at right of design areas.

As you follow directions for next two rows, look at what is happening with your yarns, as you will soon be on your own. The following review may help you think:

Leaders will be in stick shed.
They will go as far as their neighboring follower.

Followers will be in the pull shed.
They will go one individual warp more or less than their own leader, depending on the design.

These specific directions will help you through this row. Be remembering the above review as you weave.

1. Left black yarn (leader) crosses left beneath the grey and goes to left edge.

2. Brown yarn (center leader) goes left to come out in same opening as grey follower in left background. This is behind 11 front warps.

3. Right black yarn (leader) encircles edge warp and comes out with white (neighboring follower).

Just for verification, you should now have your left leader by itself at the left edge, your left follower and center leader together coming out between 28L and 29L, your center follower and right leader also together coming out between 28R and 29R, and finally your right follower alone at right edge.

This row should have given you a clear example of a leader's going as far as its neighboring follower. The next row should also be a "think row."

Row 6: PULL SHED ←: Followers only (uncross yarn pairs)

This will be the last row with specific directions during the design increase. Hereafter, you will be referring to a general outline.

1. Left grey (follower) goes to edge.

2. White (center follower) goes one individual warp more than its leader.

3. Right grey (follower) circles edge warp and goes one individual warp less than its leader.

This is a clear example of the follower's job: to go one individual warp more or less than the leader, depending on the design.

Continue on your own until the entire Coal Mine section is 1″, checking the back side for clarity but no raised edge. An outline for increasing the design follows; no warp counts are given, however.

COAL MINE OUTLINE — INCREASING DESIGN

STICK SHED →: Leaders

    1. Right black cross under, go to edge.
    2. Brown: go right. Come out at neighboring follower.
    3. Left black: cross under follower at edge. Circle side warp. Come out at neighboring follower.

PULL SHED →: Followers (uncross yarn pairs)

    1. Right grey goes to edge.
    2. White goes one individual warp more than its own leader.
    3. Left grey circles edge warp and goes one individual warp less than its own leader.

STICK SHED ←: Leaders

    1. Left black cross under. Go to edge.
    2. Brown comes out at neighboring follower.
    3. Right black goes under follower yarn, circles edge warp, comes out at neighboring follower.

PULL SHED ←: Followers (uncross yarn pairs)

    1. Left grey goes to edge.
    2. White goes one individual warp more than leader.
    3. Right grey goes one individual warp less than leader.

When Coal Mine is 1″, it will be time to expand the brown-white section clear across the weaving. Directions follow.

C. Interior Coal Mine stripe: ¼″ in design colors

When your Coal Mine section is 1″ and yarns hang at the right of your design areas, break off all yarns close to weaving. Place leaders in stick shed to left and followers in pull shed to left. Then begin your interior Coal Mine stripe.

Row 1: STICK SHED ←: Leader

Lay in brown (center leader).

Row 2: PULL SHED ←: Follower

Lay in white (center follower).

Continuing with two rows in each direction weave until this section is ¼″. This will bring your entire Coal Mine to 1¼″ which allows for future packing.

D. Coal Mine design: Decrease for 1″

Your entire Coal Mine section should now be 1¼″ high and your brown and white yarns hanging on right. Break these off near edge and again weave them into their respective sheds. Now reintroduce the background colors as follows:

Row 1: STICK SHED ←: Leaders

Lay in leaders to correspond to space occupied before the center stripe.

Row 2: PULL SHED ←: Followers

Lay in followers in same direction.
Grey to left edge.
White (center follower) 1 individual warp less than leader.
Grey (right follower) 1 individual warp more than leader.
Your diamond is now beginning to decrease. Continue until the leaders are back to their original 15-10-15 count.
Though the situation is reversed and things look slightly different, problems will be minimized if you remember:

A leader goes up to the neighboring follower.
A follower goes one individual warp more or less than its leader.
And in so doing, they both end up developing the design with each row.

A general outline for decrease follows.

61

COAL MINE OUTLINE: DECREASING DESIGN

STICK SHED →: Leaders

    1. Right black goes to right edge.

    2. Brown cross under. Come out at neighboring follower.

    3. Left black cross under follower at edge, circle edge warp, and come out at neighboring follower.

PULL SHED →: Followers (uncross yarn pairs)

    1. Right grey goes to right edge.

    2. White crosses under and goes one individual warp less than its own leader.

    3. Left grey circles edge warp and goes one individual warp more than its own leader.

STICK SHED ←: Leaders

    1. Left black goes to edge.

    2. Brown crosses under and comes out at neighboring follower.

    3. Right black goes under follower yarn, circles edge warp and comes out at neighboring follower.

PULL SHED ←: Followers (uncross yarn pairs)

    1. Left grey goes to edge.

    2. White crosses under and goes one individual warp less than its own leader.

    3. Right grey goes one individual warp more than its leader.

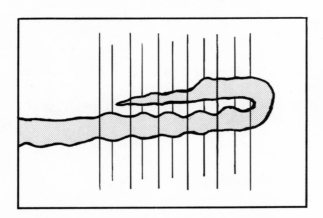

Figure 6.12: *Termination technique for Coal Mine, twill, two-faced and Crystal yarns.*

V. *Completion*

In next to last row of Coal Mine, break off leader yarn and *insert end back into stick shed* with rest of yarn (Fig. 6.12). Repeat with follower in pull shed.

The next design will be a repetition of the doubled cross (design: black; background: white). Utilize the opportunity of plain weave to fill in and re-distribute warps evenly to provide a good base for the small diamond twill that will follow.

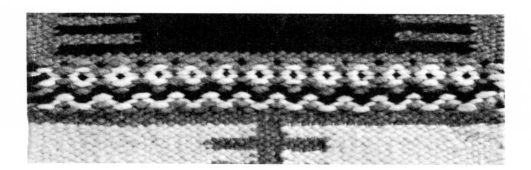

Small diamond twill

The small diamond twill, a four-shed technique, is used throughout the res-ervation. It is especially favored in saddle blankets where thickness is desirable. In this particular twill, small light diamonds with dark centers begin to stack upright. In between them, there soon appear diamonds of the third color — again with dark centers.

This easily counted, small diamond pattern provides good introduction to four-shed techniques.

I. *General understanding of the diamond twill*

Diamond twills are carried out with the aid of four shed/heddle arrange-ments, rather than the two used in regular tapestry weave. These sheds facilitate a threading of weft that is irregular. Sometimes a yarn will go over three warps, then under one, then over three, etc. This is in contrast to the constant over-one, under-one, over-one, under-one, which characterizes the tapestry weave used so far.

The counts that are required to produce a specific pattern are counted once and then transferred to shed and heddle arrangements so they can be used with ease throughout the weaving. The sequence in which sheds are used in relation to color combinations gives the desired pattern. Each side of the fabric will have a different color emphasis, and many variations of patterns can be woven from this single count.

Although not observed here, warps for a four-heddle weave are usually spaced more closely than for regular weave. This is because yarns going over multiple warps settle and pack more than usual. Saddle blankets, an item in which thickness is desirable, employ the diamond twill to good advantage.

If you are considering using the diamond twill exclusively in a weaving, try spacing warps 12 per inch (6 marks to the inch on dowels). Or if you would like a heavier weave, continue with the 8 warps per inch as usual, but use a thicker yarn for weft. Another consideration in a diamond-twill rug is that no fill-ins can occur without disrupting the pattern. For this reason, equal warp distribution is essential throughout!

II. *Project preparation*

Though the diamond twill can be used exclusively in one weaving, directions here are for a 3½″ stripe within the 10″ x 23″ sampler.

1. Since fill-ins are not possible, please do not begin your diamond twill until you have established an even weaving line and evenly distributed your warp. Additionally, if warp redistribution is difficult for you, a review might in order (p. 85 WWW).

2. You will not be using your existing shed/heddle combination for this technique. Therefore, please tie them up at the top for the duration of the twill. They can be brought down again at a future time.

3. Materials needed:
    4 willow sticks for the four sheds
    3 stick-shuttles
    3 distinct yarn colors: dark, medium and light of a uniform spin
    Soft, unpolished cotton string for heddles (8 ply)

III. *Counting the sheds*

Since this is the most difficult part of the diamond twill, send everyone "out of your hogan" that is not dedicated to helping you achieve accuracy. Once accurately counted and converted to shed/heddle arrangement, they are used with relative ease throughout the weaving. The following procedures may help with counting:

A. Hang a dark plain cloth behind the light warps to improve visibility.

B. If you are having difficulty on your own, have someone read the count to you while you carry it out.

64

C. Insert batten at weaving line where warps are held apart and visibility is the clearest.

D. After counting each row, replace batten with a stick. After all rows are finalized, convert the bottom three sticks to heddle arrangement. By leaving them as sticks during the counting, you can check each row against those preceding. Continual checking and rechecking is essential; mistakes are easily remedied if caught early.

E. Make heddles longer than usual — about 1¾" — so shed can open adequately.

The chart given on subsequent page will show the warp count for each of four sheds. Start with the top one (shed no. 4) and continue downward in sequence to shed no. 1.

1. Insert batten behind warps marked "X" clear across your warp.

2. After one shed has been counted, start the next — leaving preceding battens in place. (If you haven't enough battens for all four sheds, substitute a stick for the batten after the count has been determined.)

3. After all sheds have been counted, convert to proper arrangement as shown (Fig. 6.14). Shed no. 4, the stick shed, is on top; the three pull sheds follow beneath.

4. In making the heddles, loop the string onto your willow stick before and after each warp group crosses your batten. When a warp stands alone, it will be circled separately. After all heddles loop the willow, you may tie ends of a separate string to the tips of the willow to act as a "guard string" (see Figures 6.14 and 6.15).

IV. *General weaving instructions for small diamond twill*

Once shed and heddle rods are in position, you are ready to weave. General guidelines are given below; please read them through and apply them throughout.

1. *Weft scalloping:* Throughout the weaving lay yarn in *extra loosely* and maintain sufficient scallops so weft will pack well and cover warp completely, and edges will remain straight and true (p. 48 WWW). Remind yourself as you weave that diamond twill requires *even more* weft than regular weave.

2. *Warp spacing:* Maintaining an even weaving line is essential, as fill-ins of "valleys" are not possible. To minimize difficulty, select uniform yarn for the project. Also, pay close attention to warp spacing. Remember that when warps ease together in any area, a "hill" will result. Conversely, "valleys" occur in areas where warps have separated. Review technique for warp redistribution (p. 85 WWW and p. 9 of Chapter 1 in this book). Keep spacing even from the beginning and redistribute as necessary *with authority*.

STICK AND HEDDLE COUNT FOR SMALL DIAMOND TWILL
(X) = insert batten under these warps

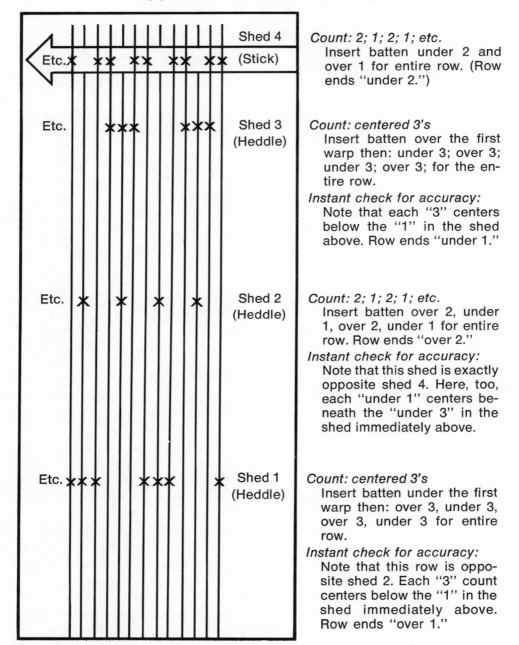

Shed 4 (Stick)

Count: 2; 1; 2; 1; etc.
Insert batten under 2 and over 1 for entire row. (Row ends "under 2.")

Shed 3 (Heddle)

Count: centered 3's
Insert batten over the first warp then: under 3; over 3; under 3; over 3; for the entire row.

Instant check for accuracy:
Note that each "3" centers below the "1" in the shed above. Row ends "under 1."

Shed 2 (Heddle)

Count: 2; 1; 2; 1; etc.
Insert batten over 2, under 1, over 2, under 1 for entire row. Row ends "over 2."

Instant check for accuracy:
Note that this shed is exactly opposite shed 4. Here, too, each "under 1" centers beneath the "under 3" in the shed immediately above.

Shed 1 (Heddle)

Count: centered 3's
Insert batten under the first warp then: over 3, under 3, over 3, under 3 for entire row.

Instant check for accuracy:
Note that this row is opposite shed 2. Each "3" count centers below the "1" in the shed immediately above. Row ends "over 1."

Figure 6.13: *Warp count for small diamond twill.*

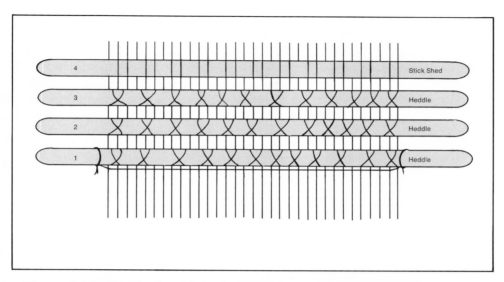

Figure 6.14: *Positioning of the four willow sticks in diamond twill. Guard string illustrated on bottom willow. (For warp count see Figure 6.13.)*

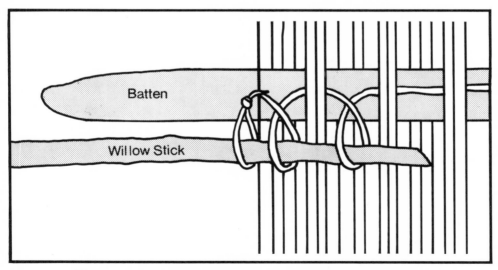

Figure 6.15: *Looping of warp groups in making heddles for 4-shed techniques.*

67

3. *Warp strumming:* When you are inserting your batten in the shed and find some warps tend to stick together, it may be helpful to strum warps (p. 43 WWW). Warp sticking is more pronounced in four-shed techniques.

4. *Circle edge warps:* When a yarn is at the side of the weaving and ready to begin a row, make special effort to circle the edge warp before inserting yarn in shed. To do this, disregard whether the edge warp is in front or behind the batten. Sometimes multiple edge warps will be circled together. This special treatment results in larger than usual loops at the selvage. The technique will be treated more specifically on following pages.

5. *Three rows — same direction:* For each row the batten will be inserted in the shed and the weft carried the full width of your weaving. There will be three rows to the left, then three to the right. Of the three, each will have a different shed and different color.

V. *Specific weaving instructions for small diamond twill*

1. Wind each of your three yarn colors on its own stick shuttle (p. 53 WWW). Since distinct shades provide for maximum design clarity, the directions that follow will use these letters to denote colors: D = dark (black); M = medium (brown); L = light (white).

2. A chart will follow to synchronize your row, shed, color and direction. It will be used throughout the small-diamond-twill section. As you preview the chart prior to actual weaving, please give special attention to sequences. Of the total 12 rows, rows 1 through 6 open the diamonds. Rows 7 through 12 close the diamonds. The weaving starts at row 1 (at the bottom) and progresses upward. The sequence is then repeated as desired.

Row	Shed	Color	Direction
12 (center)	4 (center)	D (center)	→
11	2	M	→
10	3	L	→
9	4	D	←
8	1	M	←
7	2 ⎤	L ⎤	←
6 (center)	4 ⎰ (center)	D ⎰ (center)	→
5	2 ⎦	L ⎦	→
4	1	M	→
3	4	D	←
2	3	L	←
1	2	M	← Start Here

(Close — rows 7–12; Open — rows 1–6)

68

3. Using the sequence given in the chart, your diamonds will be light with dark centers. As the sequence is repeated, medium diamonds with dark centers will appear in the spaces.

4. Specific weaving instructions for the first 6 rows will guide you initially. Please weave each row thoughtfully so that once directions end you will be able to continue.

VI. *Directions for first 6 rows*

You are now ready to weave

Please refer to the chart on the previous page so you will be familiar with its symbols once directions end.

Row 1: Shed 2 ←   Color: M (medium)

1. Shed 2: Position shed and heddle sticks. Push top two sticks up out of way and the bottom one down to isolate shed 2.

2. Pull shed 2 forward and insert batten directly behind heddles; turn on edge.

3. Insert shuttle with medium yarn into shed beneath all willows (right to left). Make large scallops and beat into place.

Row 2: Shed 3 ←   Color: L (light)

1. Shed 3: Position shed and heddle sticks. Push top stick up out of way. Push two lower ones down to isolate third one.

2. Pulling shed 3 forward to open, insert batten behind heddles and turn on edge.

3. Insert shuttle bearing light yarn into shed below all willow sticks (right to left). Scallop and beat.

Row 3: Shed 4 ←   Color: D (dark)

1. Shed 4: Position shed and heddle sticks. Push all four sticks close together at top of weaving.

2. Insert batten below all willow sticks (as in regular stick shed) and turn on edge.

3. Lay in dark yarn (right to left). Scallop and beat.

Please reread the General Weaving Instructions, paying special attention to the fourth item which explains the circling of edge warps. The following three rows will elaborate upon this principle. Thereafter you and the chart will be on your own!

Row 4: Shed 1 →   Color: M

1. Shed 1: Position shed and heddle sticks by pushing top three sticks up out of way. Pull lower one forward to open shed.

2. Insert batten directly behind heddles and turn on edge.

3. Notice that the medium yarn comes out of the weaving in front of the left edge warp. Note also that the open shed holds that same warp forward. To insert yarn directly into shed would result in left edge warp being left out (uncircled). Thus it is necessary to *circle around behind the left edge warp before entering the medium yarn into the shed.* (You will then be beginning your row behind the first four warps.)

Row 5: Shed 2 →   Color: L

1. Position shed and heddle sticks for shed 2.

2. Notice that the light yarn comes out of the weaving behind the left edge warp and that the open shed now holds that same yarn back. It is only necessary to insert yarn directly into open shed and left warp will be circled.

Row 6: Shed 4 →   Color: D

1. Position shed and heddle sticks for shed 4.

2. Notice that the dark yarn comes out of the weaving behind the left edge warp. Note also that the open shed is holding the same warp forward. Inserting yarn directly into shed would result in left edge warp uninvolved (uncircled). Thus it is necessary to *pass in front of that warp before going into shed.*

You are now on your own. Refer to the chart for shed, color and direction of row. In addition, be sure to look at how each yarn comes out of the weaving and then direct its route so that the edge warp is circled.

VII. *Variations of the small diamond twill*

Many variations are possible by manipulating shed order and color combinations. Some of these are given below.

1. *Mini-diamonds* may stack upon each other by repeating the 12-row sequence.

2. *Waves of three colors* may follow upon each other by keeping a constant shed order (i.e. 1, 2, 3, 4) and a constant color order. Waves may be started at any time, however, if you are starting waves after the 12-row sequence, use these combinations: 2M; 3L; 4D; 1M; 2L; 3D; 4M; 1L; 2D; 3M; 4L; 1D. Repeat as long as waves are desired (Fig. 6.16).

3. *Connecting circles with dark interiors* may be created using the above waves as a base. At the point that a medium-colored wave is completed, reverse shed and corresponding color combination (Fig. 6.17).

4. *Elongated circles* are also a variation of the waves. At the point that a dark wave is completed, repeat the last three sheds (counting the one just used) in their same order and with their same colors. A continued repetition

70

of the same three sheds and three colors produce verticals in those colors which elongate the design (Fig. 6.18).

Figure 6.16: *Small diamond twill variation: waves of three colors.*

Figure 6.17: *Small diamond twill variation: connecting circles.*

Figure 6.18: *Small diamond twill variation: elongated circles.*

VIII. *Completion*

In final three rows of small diamond twill, break off each color as it ends row and *insert tip back* into row with rest of yarn (Fig. 6.12).

Larger diamonds of a different look may be created by using 24-row sequences such as the one following. Here the first number indicates the row, the second number is the shed, and the letter is the color.

24-row sequence: 1-2D, 2-3L, 3-4M, 4-1D, 5-2L, 6-3M, 7-4D, 8-1L, 9-2M, 10-3D, 11-4L, 12-1M, 13-2D, 14-1M, 15-4L, 16-3D, 17-2M, 18-1L, 19-4D, 20-3M, 21-2L, 22-1D, 23-4M, 24-3L.

Try experimenting even further on your own. Use just rows 1-21, or make color changes. The possibilities will seem endless!

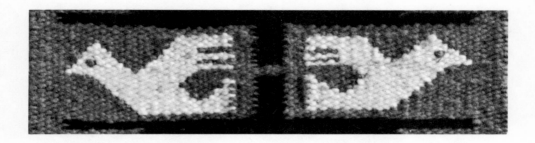

Pictorial

Pictorial rugs incorporate designs extracted from the weaver's environment. The inspiration may be nature, a child's coloring book, coins, wrappings or commercial products. Abstracted depictions amenable to the woven form are shown throughout this book.

Pictorials are usually done in the turned-joint technique, allowing the weaver greater freedom and precision in contouring. A review of Chapter 3 may be helpful.

The birds charted here (Fig. 6.19) are central to the sampler. Please remember as you weave them that the design you make may turn out taller or shorter than the one drawn here.

Variables of many types come into play during weaving. Warp spacing, weft size, and how hard you pack all influence proportions. Just feel free to innovate and elaborate as situations occur, enjoying the spontaneity inherent in the pictorial approach!

THE DIAGONAL

When you are forming the diagonals of the birds using the turned joint, the technique is the same as in the doubled cross. The same rule applies as to which yarn to use first. So does the one about including the front warp but not the back as you form your design. The only thing different is the diagonal. Here counts change gradually and continually instead of abruptly. In this regard, the pictorial is closely akin to the Coal Mine. The smooth diagonal formed by going one individual warp further each row is the same as in the Coal Mine. So is the angle.

To begin, use the first row to lay yarns in, thus establishing the beginning count. In each row thereafter, just go one warp further or less to develop the diagonal in the direction of the design. *Do not worry if wefts turn around adjacent warps rather than the same one. In the next row the turning warp will move and the overlap will occur.* For a close-up view of how the smooth diagonal looks row by row, please refer to Figure 3.3, p. 20.

Total width of this design: four inches

1 inch · 2 inches · 1 inch

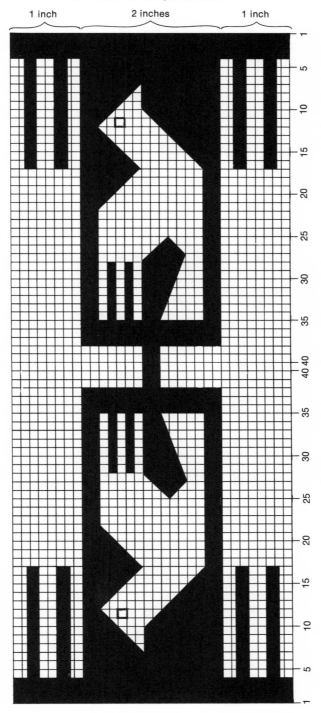

Figure 6.19: *Pictorial charted: double birds.*

In certain places (i.e. top of bird tail) you will want an even shallower angle. In these instances it may be necessary to sidestep *two* individual warps instead of just one.

Since the design will be changing continually, some beginners find it helpful to temporarily mark the turning warp by loosely tying a piece of string to it about 8″ above your weaving. Once your design is set up, you will be changing the turning warp after it has been circled twice (once by each color).

If in the process of trying this technique, you find you are not achieving a smooth diagonal, you might want to take it all out and then consider simplifying. One possibility here is removing the verticals between the birds. Or simply weave *one* bird as per Figure 6.20.

Figure 6.20: *Pictorial charted: single bird.*

If the irregularity of the angles is still too difficult, you might consider a modified Crystal design such as illustrated in Figure 6.21. To get you started, specific weaving instructions are given.

As you weave, be assured that it is always difficult to pick up a new technique and that practice alone can make it yours to use with ease and confidence. Approach the design with a sense of trial, error, observation, learning and determination. The skills you learn here can bring you much satisfaction and enjoyment, for they open to you a new world of available designs!

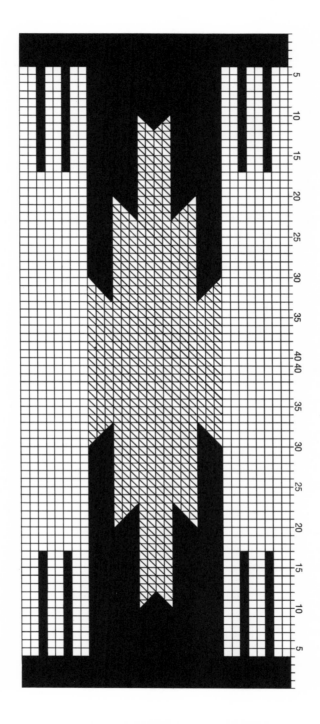

Figure 6.21: *Crystal design charted.*

CRYSTAL DESIGN (using the turned joint)

Row 1: STICK SHED ←

Begin by marking your turning warps: TW-30L and Tw-30R.
1. Lay in left yarn behind 15 front warps.
2. Lay in center yarn behind 10 front warps.
3. Lay in right yarn behind 15 front warps.

Row 2: PULL SHED →

1. TW-R → Edge. Enter shed at TW-30R (back warp; ignore). Move marker 1 warp to left. 31R becomes new turning warp.*
2. TW-L → TW-R. Enter shed at TW-L. (It's in front of batten.) Include by circling around behind it before entering shed. Come out at 31R (front warp; include).
3. Edge → TW-L. Insert yarn at edge and come out at 30L (in front; include).

Row 3: STICK SHED ←

1. Edge ← TW-L. Left TW is in back; ignore. Since TW-L has been circled twice, move marker 1 warp to R. 31L is new TW.
2. TW-L ← TW-R. TW-R is in back; ignore. Come out at new TW-L (a front warp; include).
3. TW-R ← Edge. Ignore TW-R.

Row 4: PULL SHED →

1. TW-R → Edge. Include TW-R. Move marker to new TW 32R.
2. TW-L → TW-R. Ignore both TWs.
3. Edge → TW-L. Ignore TW-L.

Row 5: STICK SHED ←

1. Edge ← T-L. Include TW-L. Move marker to 32L.
2. TW-L ← TW-R. Include TW-R. Ignore TW-L.
3. TW-R ← Edge. Include TW-R.

Row 6: PULL SHED →

1. TW-R → Edge. Ignore TW-R. Move marker to 33R.
2. TW-L → TW-R. Include TW-L and TW-R.
3. Edge → TW-L. Include TW-L.

---

* In initiating or changing a design, a turning warp may be moved *after a single turn*. This brings into focus the rule: *the decreasing-shape yarn circles the warp first.*

Continue on your own until design is ⅜" and yarns are on right. Then change your design to TW-20 L and R. Follow the directions given here substituting 20 for 30. When design is again ⅜" your turning warp will change to 10. Again substitute your new numbers in the basic directions, reaching the half of your design after just ¼". At this point you will be reversing your diagonals to complete the Crystal design.

Medium diamond twill

There are many variations on the diamond twill, the three basic counts given in the book being but an introduction to the whole. If you find this particular four-shed technique fascinating, you might enjoy seeing a very complex double saddle blanket woven in 1942. An illustration of this lovely weaving is in *Navajo Weaving Today.** Or if you would enjoy weaving a complete rug in diamond twill, you might think in terms of the two-faced diamond twill as a next project.

I. *General understanding of the diamond twill*

To acquire a general understanding of the diamond twill, please turn to the Small Diamond Twill section where descriptions are detailed. Thereafter, continue here for additional considerations.

If you are using the diamond twill exclusively in a weaving, be certain to determine the width of your proposed project by multiples of diamond units. For example, a proposed 30-inch saddle blanket in this particular pattern would need 236 warps at 8 per inch. (This would provide 9 diamond units

*Bertha P. Dutton, Museum of New Mexico Press, 1961. Cover and p. 34 of original printing. 19

of 26 warps each plus a beginning and ending warp to create an actual woven width of 29½".) On the other hand, if you are warping 12 per inch, use 366 warps (183 marks on dowel no. 2) to make 14 diamond units between your beginning and ending warps, and an actual woven size of 30½".

II. *Materials needed:*

  4 willow sticks for the four sheds
  3 stick shuttles
  3 distinct and uniformly spun yarns: dark, medium, light
  Soft, unpolished cotton string for heddles (8 ply)

III. *Project preparation*

Please refer back to the Small Diamond Twill section for general instructions in *counting the sheds.* Then continue here for an overview of the actual count.

A. The overview and count

All four sheds are drawn together (Fig. 6.22) to help you visualize the total effect and the diamond formation. On subsequent pages directions will be given for counting each shed separately. Before proceeding please note that:

  1. Pairs (XX) move over one individual warp in each shed.
  2. Alternate sheds are opposite.
  3. This diamond twill is calculated to center 3 diamonds across the 10" weaving. Since the count is based on 80 individual warps, the whole design is one warp off-center to the left.

Having the general concept in mind, please begin now to count each of the sheds. Detailed directions follow.

B. Individual shed counts

  1. Shed 4: STICK SHED

This is basically a "2-warps-in-front, 2-warps-in-back" count with a deviation of "3 warps in front" which occurs at the center and ends of each diamond. Insert your batten right to left in shed according to the count in Figure 6.22. Start with the "starting warp" at the right, and proceed with the sequence. Repeat the sequence two more times (a total of three) and finish with the "ending warp" on the left. When your batten is in place, recount for accuracy. Then replace batten with one willow stick and push it up to the top of the way. Proceed then with shed 3.

  2. Shed 3: PULL SHED

This is basically a "2-warps-in-front, 2-warps-behind" count with a devi-

78

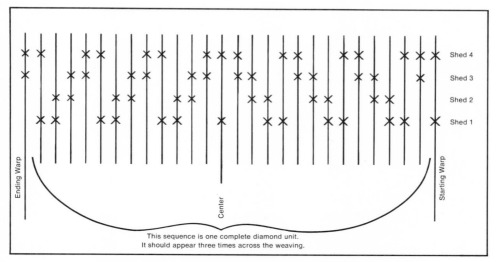

Figure 6.22: *Medium diamond twill warp count.*
(X) = insert batten behind these warps.

ation of "1 warp behind" occuring at the center of the diamond and a "1 warp in front" at each end.

Insert your batten right to left in shed according to the count in Figure 6.22. Start with the "starting warp" at the right and proceed with the sequence. Repeat the sequence two more times (a total of three) and finish with the ending warp on the left.

3. Shed 2: PULL SHED

This is the opposite of shed 4. Continue with the basic 2-2-2-2 count and deviate with "3 warps behind" at the center and ends of each diamond. Check this count against shed 4 to see if they are exactly opposite, then proceed to shed 1 below.

4. Shed 1: PULL SHED

This is the opposite of shed 3. Continue with the basic 2-2-2-2 count and deviate with "1 warp in front" at the center of each diamond, and "1 warp in back" at each end. Check this count against shed 3 to see that they are exactly opposite. Then convert all counts to heddle arrangements (pp. 40, 41 WWW), remembering to loop string onto willow sticks before and after warp *units* (Fig. 6.15, p. 67).

IV. *General weaving instructions for the medium diamond twill*

Please review general weaving instructions in Small Diamond Twill.

79

V. *Specific weaving instructions for the medium diamond twill*

A. Wind each of your three yarn colors on its own stick shuttle (p. 53 WWW). Since distinct shades provide for maximum design clarity and facilitate learning, the directions that follow use these letters to denote colors: D = dark (black); M = medium (brown); L = light (white).

B. The chart below synchronizes your row, shed, color and direction. It will be used throughout the Medium Diamond Twill section. As you preview the chart prior to your actual weaving, please give special attention to the following rhythms:

1. Note that a 12-row sequence is given and that you will start at the bottom with row 1 to open the diamonds. Reversal of the 12 rows closes them.

2. Note that the shed sequence proceeds 1-2-3-4 and repeats three times. (You can think of this as climbing a ladder.)

3. Note that the color sequence proceeds light, medium, dark and repeats four times. Again this is a constant progression.

DIRECTIONS FOR FIRST SIX ROWS

Please refer to the chart below so you will be familiar with its symbols once directions end.

Row 1: Shed 1 ←   Color: L (light)

1. Shed 1 — Position shed and heddle sticks: Push top three sticks up out of way. Pull lower one forward to make shed.

		Row	Shed	Color	Direction
Closes Diamonds	Opens Diamonds	12	4 ⎤	D ⎤	→
		11	3 ⎱	M ⎰	→
		10	2 ⎰	L ⎱	→
		9	1 ⎦	D ⎦	←
		8	4 ⎤	M ⎤	←
		7	3 ⎱	L ⎰	←
		6	2 ⎰	D ⎤	→
		5	1 ⎦	M ⎰	→
		4	4 ⎤	L ⎦	→
		3	3 ⎱	D ⎤	←
		2	2 ⎰	M ⎰	←
		1	1 ⎦	L ⎦	◄— Start Here

Medium diamond twill: Weaving Chart for one full sequence.

2. Insert batten directly behind heddles and turn on edge.

3. Lay in light yarn for full row (right to left). Beat in place.

Row 2: Shed 2 ←   Color: M (medium)

1. Shed 2 — Position shed and heddle sticks: Push top two sticks up out of way. With bottom two together, pull just no. 2 forward.

2. Insert batten directly below all shed rods and turn on edge.

3. Lay in medium yarn for full row (right to left). Beat in place.

Row 3: Shed 3 ←   Color: D (dark)

1. Shed 3 — Position shed and heddle sticks: Push top stick up out of way. Push two lower ones down, to isolate third one.

2. Two battens may be used to facilitate shed 3: Pulling 3 forward to open shed, insert alternate batten *behind* heddles. Turn on edge. Next insert regular batten below all shed rods as before; turn on edge.

3. Lay in dark yarn for full row (right to left). Beat in place.

Please *reread the General Weaving Instructions,* paying special attention to the fourth item which explains the circling of edge warps. The following three rows will elaborate upon this principle. Thereafter you and the chart will be on your own!

Row 4: Shed 4 →   Color: L

1. Shed 4 — Position shed and heddle sticks: Push all sticks close together at top of weaving.

2. Insert batten below all sticks and turn on edge.

3. Notice that light yarn comes out of weaving in front of the left edge warp. Thus, it is only necessary to *insert yarn directly into open shed,* and the left warp will automatically be circled.

Row 5: Shed 1 →   Color: M

1. Position shed and heddle sticks for shed 1.

2. Notice that the medium yarn comes out of the weaving in front of left edge warp. It is therefore necessary to *cross behind that warp,* before going into the shed. (Weft will thus begin this row under three individual warps.)

Row 6: Shed 2 →   Color: D

1. Position shed and heddle sticks for shed 2.

2. Notice that since the dark yarn comes out of the weaving *behind* the left edge warp, and the batten is now holding this warp back, all that is necessary is for the yarn to enter the shed directly and the edge warp will be included.

You are now on your own. Refer to the chart for shed, color and direction of each row.

In addition, be sure to look at how each yarn that you are using comes out of the weaving. Next look where it will be going. Then, as necessary, direct its route so the edge warp is circled.

Throughout your weaving keep in mind that rows 1 through 12 open the diamonds. To close them, the color/shed sequence may be reversed at any point.

VI. *Variations of the medium diamond twill*

A. Diamonds may follow one upon the other by alternately opening and closing the 12-row sequence.

B. *Large diamonds* are made by opening the sequence twice and then closing it twice.

C. *Zig-zags* may be created by continually opening the sequence.

D. *Verticals* may be interspersed with diamonds at two points:

1. *When diamonds are open*

Open diamonds by ascending the sequence of rows 1 through 12. Then, to create veritcals in three colors (Fig. 6.23), repeat rows 10, 11, and 12 as many times as desired, using the corresponding shed/color combinations in the chart.

2. *When diamonds are closed*

Close diamonds by descending the sequence. Then create verticals (Fig. 6.24) by repeating rows 3, 2 and 1 as many times as desired, using the corresponding shed/color combinations in the chart.

Figure 6.23: *Medium diamond twill variation:
verticals begun with diamonds open.*

Figure 6.24: *Medium diamond twill variation:*
verticals begun with diamonds closed.

E. Openings, closings and verticals can be combined in a variety of ways to create interesting designs. One such combination is offered in Figure 6.25 and requires approximately 4" for the total effect.

VI. *Completion*

In the three final rows of the medium diamond twill, break off each color as it ends the row and insert tip back into row with rest of yarn (Fig. 6.12, p. 62).

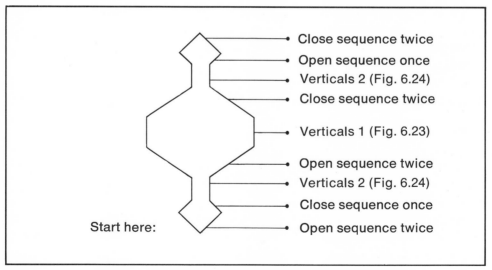

Close sequence twice
Open sequence once
Verticals 2 (Fig. 6.24)
Close sequence twice

Verticals 1 (Fig. 6.23)

Open sequence twice
Verticals 2 (Fig. 6.24)
Close sequence once
Start here: Open sequence twice

Figure 6.25: *Medium diamond twill variation:*
verticals, openings, and closings combined.

83

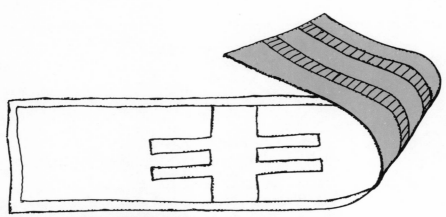

Two-faced: the doubled cross

By now you have repeated the doubled-cross motif many times and may be ready for a variation on the theme. If energy and adventurous spirit are willing, I suggest you render the same motif in the *two-faced technique.* The front side of your weaving will appear with the regular doubled-cross design. The back side, however, will be completely different — stripes of whatever colors you choose. Trying this small section in the sampler will serve to introduce you to the two-faced approach. If you find it appealing, you may want to try a whole weaving in the technique later. Chapter 7 tells you how.

If, at this point, your energy is waning however, simply repeat the doubled cross in the regular weave.

I. *Concept of the two-faced*

The two-faced is an advanced technique in which four sheds are manipulated to render one design on the front, and another on the back. A thicker than usual weaving results.

II. *Considerations*

Color: Whenever you are embarking on a two-faced, select colors carefully. Try to put brighter colors on the front-side design and duller ones on the reverse. This way the small flecks of color that show through the design will be negligible.

Back-side Design: As you begin to understand the two-faced, be giving some thought to how you'd like the back side to look. It can be stripes of any width and in various techniques such as Coal Mine or Crystal. In considering either of these, however, be advised that the "stitches" are larger than usual in this technique (more on this later). Thus, Coal Mine vertical pinstriping will be broader than usual, as will the Crystal "waves" (see p. 88).

III. *Materials needed*

4 willow sticks for the four sheds

Soft, unpolished cotton string for heddles (8 ply)

White and black weft for the front side; your choice of muted shades for the reverse (brown, grey?)

IV. *Counting the sheds*

The counts for the two-faced technique are given below. Please transfer them to shed and heddle arrangements according to directions in the Small Diamond Twill chapter.

STICK SHED AND HEDDLE COUNT FOR THE TWO-FACED TECHNIQUE
(X) = insert batten under these warps

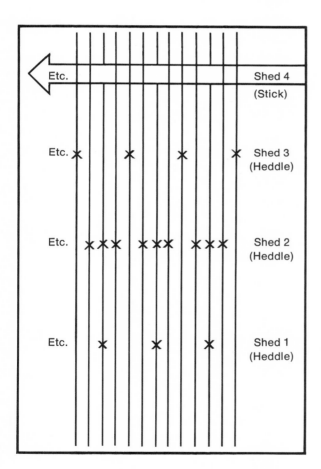

Shed 4 (Stick)

Count: over 1; under 3
Insert batten over 1 and under 3 for entire row noting exceptions where the row begins "under 2" and ends "over 2."

Shed 3 (Heddle)

Count: under 1; over 3
Insert batten under 1 and then over 3 for the row. Each "under 1" centers directly below the "under 3" in the shed above. Row ends "over 3."

Shed 2 (Heddle)

Count: over 1; under 3
Insert batten over 1 and under 3 for the row. Note that the "over 1" centers directly below the "under 1" in the previous shed, and that these two sheds are opposite. Row ends "under 3."

Shed 1 (Heddle)

Count: under 1; over 3
Insert batten under 1 and over 3 for the row. Note that the "under 1" is directly below the center warp in the 3 count above. Note too that this shed is opposite shed 4. The row begins "over 2" and ends "under 2."

Figure 6.26: *Warp count for two-faced technique.*

V. *Understanding the two-faced technique*

If you will study the shed counts on the preceding page, you will see that sheds 1 and 3 put most of the yarn on the front side of the weaving — they go "over 3" except for an occasional "under 1" all across their rows. The opposite is true of sheds 2 and 4. Here, most of the yarn skips along the back side, only occasionally latching onto a warp. With some thought you can see that when you insert a white yarn in shed 1, it will appear as long front stitches. The back side, however, will show small occasional stitches. If a grey yarn follows in shed 2, it will then slide down *behind* the white to cover those small white specks that showed on the back.

The alternation of shed 1 with 2, of shed 3 with 4, will form the basis for the two-faced technique. One row will be a front yarn, the second a back.

An additional concept also comes into play here. Since sheds 1 and 3 control the front side with larger-than-usual stitches, you can see that only half the number of warps that regularly cross the batten in a shed are now available to use as turning warps in the front-side design!

VI. *Charting the two-faced technique*

As in the doubled-cross section of the sampler, warps will be counted individually and numbered according to their location on the right or left side of the weaving. Therefore TW 38L indicates that your turning warp is the 38th warp on the left of your weaving.

In most charts, half the number of warps (those that cross the batten) are drawn. In Figure 6.27 warps have been cut in half again! Only the number available as turning warps in sheds 1 and 3 are drawn. Note, too, that alternate lines are dark, indicating warps that are forward in shed 1. The alternate light lines denote front warps in shed 3.

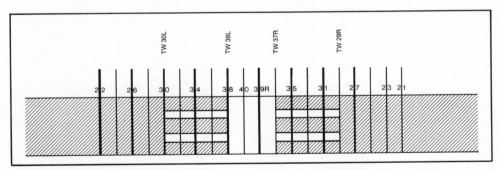

Figure 6.27: *Doubled-cross motif charted in two-faced technique. (Dark warp lines indicate front warps in shed 1. Alternate light warp lines indicate front warps in shed 3.)*

86

VII. *General weaving instructions for the two-faced technique*

The concepts outlined in the last section will become clearer upon application. Once sheds are in place, prepare to weave. Please keep in mind that this is a four-shed technique and that some of the same principles apply as in the twill. It is very important to *lay weft in loosely;* the two-faced consumes enormous amounts. Also, be certain to keep warps evenly distributed; once again there will be no fill-ins. And finally, the special circling of edge warps in the twill are also encountered here. If any of these principles need review, please reread those sections in the Small Diamond Twill chapter.

VIII. *Specific weaving instructions for the two-faced doubled-cross motif*

Row 1: SHED 1 ← Lay in front design yarns in following order:

1. White begins at 38L and goes to left edge.
2. Black goes behind 39R and 38L.
3. White starts at right edge and comes out to left of 35R.

Row 2: SHED 2 ←

Lay in a muted back yarn that will slide down behind previous row.

Row 3: SHED 3 → Continue front design yarns in the following order:

1. White yarn goes around TW 37R and into shed (it's in front; include). It goes to right edge.
2. Black goes into shed (TW 38L is in back; ignore). It comes out to right of TW 37R (front warp; include).
3. White yarn circles edge warp and comes out to right of 36L (TW 38L is in back; ignore).

Row 4: SHED 4 →

Insert back yarn that will slide down behind previous row.

Row 5: SHED 1 ← Front design

1. White yarn around behind 38L (front; include).
2. Black into shed behind 2 warps.
3. White comes out left of 35R. (TW 37R is in back; ignore.)

Continue rows 2 through 5 until two-faced is ¼". Then change your design count as usual.

IX. *Completion*

As you develop your two-faced, be sure to keep the weaving line even and warps well distributed to provide a good base for the Crystal technique to follow. Small stripes tend to emphasize any unevenness of the weaving line that exists. In the final four rows of the two-faced, break off each color as it ends the row and insert tip back into row along with rest of yarn (Fig. 6.12, p. 62).

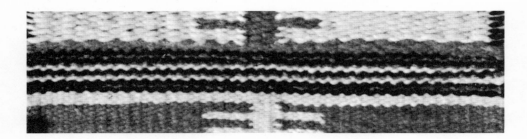

Crystal

The Crystal technique, characterized by stripes of wavy lines, is woven mainly in an area of the reservation known as Crystal — hence the name. The stripes are often separated by areas of design — all in strong, plant-dyed hues. When these colors are alternated to form the undulating pattern, the total effect is strong, rich, and very lovely.

I. *The project*

The wavy lines of the Crystal rugs are achieved simply by weaving alternate colors two rows each (left then right).

To achieve a Crystal effect in two colors:
Row 1: Lay in light yarn in stick shed ←.
Row 2: Return it in pull shed →. Leave at side.
Row 3: Lay in dark yarn in stick shed ←.
Row 4: Return it in pull shed →. Leave at side.
Row 5 onward: Repeat rows 1 through 4 as desired.

To achieve a Crystal effect in three colors: Though more than two colors is not traditionally Crystal, more can be rotated by breaking each and re-threading the end before beginning another color.

Figure 6.28: *Variety of Crystal design possibilities.*

Crystal designs are used in alternation with the wavy lines. Usually based on the flat diagonal, they are done with the turned-joint technique (Chapter 3).

If you would like to do an entire rug in Crystal, you might utilize one of the designs in Figure 6.28. Or if your plans are more monumental, consider the large Crystal designs charted in Chapter 5.

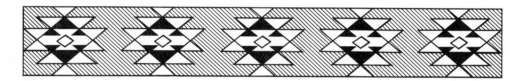

II. *Completion of Crystal*

Crystal yarns can be terminated by breaking each color off as it ends the row and inserting the top back into same shed along with rest of yarn (Fig. 6.12). The next design will be your final doubled cross, this time a white cross against a brown background.

III. *Completion of entire sampler*

As you approach the top of your sampler, give some thought to how you will be displaying your weaving. *If it will be flat* (on a table, for instance) then proceed according to sampler design, tufting the last inch before the top 1½″ border. *If it will be hung* the design may be reproportioned to allow for hanging tufts (to expose more of the two-faced and Crystal). One reproportionment is offered here:

     Crystal section: expand from 1″ to 1½″.

     Doubled-cross motif: 1″ as before.

     Tufting: 1″ as in bottom stripe.

This leaves 1″ for top border in which to rhythmically and patiently complete the whole.

CHAPTER 7

Look Beyond

TO MANY NAVAJO WEAVERS, the ultimate in weaving mastery is knowing the two-faced technique. Since relatively few women do know it, these rugs have long been considered a collector's item. Two projects are offered here, and I think both will provide you with bountiful challenge and satisfaction.

The two-faced diamond twill

The two-faced diamond twill is a four-shed weaving in which front and back sides are strikingly different. In it, stripes of variegated diamonds outline blocks of solid color — red on the front, brown on the back (Fig. 7.1).

Capitalizing on the thickness of weave and the contrasting front and back sides, many weavers consider enlarging the project to 30" x 30" saddle blanket dimensions. Some ideas on this follow:

I. *Size*

The project described here is 23½" wide by 24" long. The specific width is based on complete diamond units, but can be broadened by using double diamonds in the interior, or adding multiples of four warps in the block areas. The length can be extended to whatever your loom will accommodate.

II. *Materials needed*

4 additional willow sticks for the 4 sheds, including a thick (½") one for the stick shed
3 stick shuttles

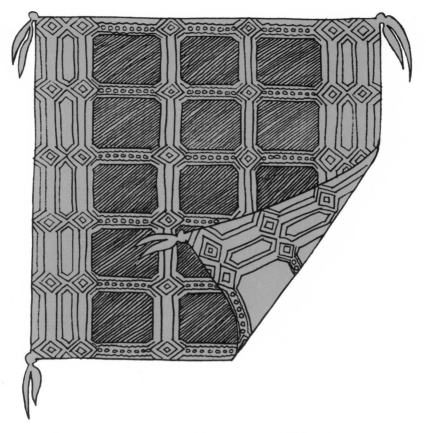

Figure 7.1: *The two-faced diamond twill showing strips of varie-gated diamonds outlining distinctly different color blocks on front and back.*

Soft, unpolished cotton string for heddles (8 ply)
130 yards warp
3 weft colors uniformly spun (for four-shed techniques such as this, weft should be heavier than usual): 1 lb. dark red; 1 lb. natural brown; ¼ lb. off-white or wheat
Two 110″ two-ply edging cords. Red is suggested.

III. *Warping particulars*

For the 23½″ x 24″ project you will need 94 marks on *both* top and bottom dowels (189 individual warps). This means that your beginning knot will be on dowel no. 1 and your ending knot will be on dowel no. 2. These dowels will be 22½″ apart on the warping frame to afford the 24″ project length.

91

Mount your warp on the loom as usual leaving the willow sticks tied together (the lower one *unconverted* to heddle arrangement).

IV. *Counting the sheds of the two-faced diamond twill*

While counting the sheds for this technique, push the willow sticks inserted during warping up to the top third of your warp and count below them. These sticks will help maintain warp sequence during counting and can be removed when all sheds are accurately in place. Also, be sure to count each successive warp separately — not just those in front of the batten as in the hooked-joint technique.

There are additional and essential suggestions given in the "Small Diamond Twill" chapter that will help you count your sheds accurately and convert the count to shed/heddle arrangement. Please read them at this time (pp. 64, 65, 67).

The count for the two-faced diamond twill is given in Figure 7.2 below. Place your batten behind those warps marked "X." When you reach the warp labeled "center warp," reverse the count for the rest of the row. (You can turn the page upside down and continue to the left on the same row.)

V. *General weaving instructions for the two-faced diamond twill*

The weaving instructions given in the "Small Diamond Twill" chapter are again pertinent here. As an addendum to no. 5 ("Three rows — same direction"), please note that this is true in the diamond twill section of your design. However, in the two-faced section, just two colors are used, red going over and back in sheds 2 and 3, brown following over and back in sheds 4 and 1. Charts for the twill and two-faced sections follow on the facing page.

VI. *Specific weaving instructions*

1. Wind each of your three yarn colors on its own stick shuttle (p. 52

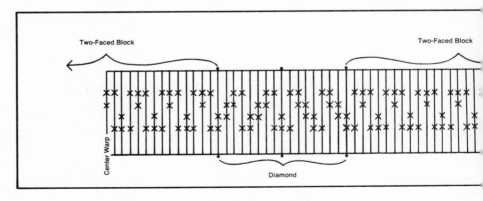

Figure 7.2: *Warp count for two-faced diamond twill.*

Weaving Chart for Diamond Twill Stripe

		Row	Shed	Color	Direction
Close Diamonds	Open Diamonds	23	3	R	→
		22	2	B	→
		21	1	W	←
		20	4	R	←
		19	3	B	←
		18	2	W	→
		17	1	R	→
		16	4	B	→
		15	3	W	←
		14	2	R	←
		13	1	B	←
		12	4	W	→
		11	3	R	→
		10	2	B	→
		9	1	W	←
		8	4	R	←
		7	3	B	←
		6	2	W	→
		5	1	R	→
		4	4	B	→
		3	3	W	←
		2	2	R	←
		1	1	B	←

Weaving Chart for Two-Faced Blocks

Row	Shed	Color
4	4	B
3	3	R
2	2	R
1	1	B

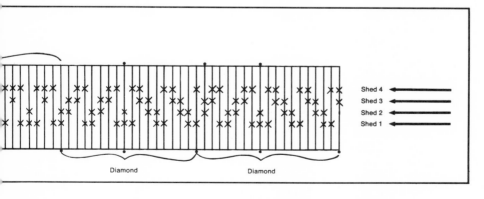

Shed 4
Shed 3
Shed 2
Shed 1

Diamond   Diamond

(X) = insert batten behind these warps.

WWW). The directions that follow use these letters to denote colors: R = deep red; B = natural brown; and W = off-white or wheat.

2. Use red yarn for the first four rows in which yarn envelops alternate warp pairs. Additionally, increase weft scallops as this technique requires even looser rows than usual.

3. Since filling in of "valleys" is not possible, it is important to keep warps evenly spaced throughout (p. 85 WWW). Additionally, use a light fork beat so that color blocks and twill sections will pack uniformly.

4. The weaving chart on the preceding page synchronizes your row: the shed you will use, the color of your yarn, and the direction you will be going. It will be used throughout the weaving. As you preview the chart prior to your actual weaving, give special attention to the following sequences:

a. Note that a 23-row sequence is given and that you begin at the bottom with row 1 and *proceed upward* to row 23. This opens the diamonds.

b. Reversal of sequence — rows 22 through 1 — closes the diamonds.

c. The shed sequence proceeds 1, 2, 3, 4, and repeats six times.

d. The color sequence begins Brown, Red, Wheat and repeats the same order seven times.

5. Begin your project by weaving rows 1 through 23 and then 22 through 1 to form your first stripe of twill. Done correctly diamonds will be joined together by a series of wavy lines that center a row of red dots as the sequence reverses. (After row 23, disregard direction of rows in the chart — just continuing 3 in each direction.)

6. Begin colored blocks: When first stripe of diamonds is complete, discontinue wheat yarn by breaking to ½″ end and inserting it back into same shed (Fig. 6.13). It is time to begin your blocks of color using the "Weaving Chart for Two-Faced Blocks." As you make the transition from diamonds to blocks please note that the final row of diamonds uses brown in shed 1. This is the same combination as used in the first row of blocks *and should not be repeated.*

Repeat rows 1–4 several times. Done correctly, red blocks will be separated by verticals above the diamonds. And you will want to look at the back side of your weaving to delight in the appearance of *brown* blocks of color.

7. Calculate your design spacing: When you are well into your first block, pause and calculate about how large your blocks will be so as to distribute six diamonds and five blocks within your 24″ weaving length. The pattern drawn here is calculated on stripes being 1½″ each and blocks 3″ each. It is best to use these dimensions as a rough estimate *only* and base *your* design on what you have just woven and your actual warp length. Dimensions will vary from weaver to weaver according to individual warping tension, warp spacing, weft size and heaviness of packing.

94

8. Finishing: Once you have completed your second diamond sequence, give a thought to how you plan to finish your rug. Some weavers prefer to weave the top row of diamonds at this time, and then continue the rest of the rug as usual. The advantage to this method is that finishing is then accomplished in a block-area where warp-count is less complex. If this is your preference, simply reposition stick shed below all heddles. Then, using the new arrangement, weave the top diamonds, pushing rows upward. (Since sheds are reordered, it may be helpful temporarily to label each willow stick as to shed number.) When diamond is complete, reposition stick-shed as before and resume upward growth.

When you reach the top, finishing will be much as usual — slow! After shed-stick is removed, you can put in two yarns with each row — one up and one down (p. 78 WWW). Umbrella ribs are especially useful here as weft crosses the entire weaving. Keep each heddle in until no longer useful. When all are removed you will be using a sacking needle to finish your rug in the block-area as mentioned. You can refer to the count chart as needed and then to the summary page of the Two-Faced Morning Star design for inspiration.

The two-faced "morning star" design

In the two-faced technique, four shed/heddle combinations are manipulated to render one design on the front of the fabric, and an entirely different one (usually stripes) on the back side. The result is a thick fabric and a marvelous challenge in concept!

I. *Preparation*

The two-faced technique has much in common with the diamond twill, both requiring manipulation of four sheds. For this reason, please review two sections in the small diamond twill instructions: Counting the Sheds points a, b, d, and e; and General Weaving Instructions points 1 through 4.

Since this particular design employs the turned joint, it is recommended that the weaver have knowledge of and ease with this technique prior to undertaking the "Morning Star" design. It would also be useful to review the general concepts and rules that govern this technique in Chapter 3.

Finally, be giving some thought as to how you'd like the back side of your weaving to look. It can be stripes of any width and in various techniques, such as Coal Mine or Crystal.

If considering the former, be advised that the vertical pinstriping will be broader than usual, as "stitches" are larger than usual in this technique. Additional explanation follows in the "Understanding" section of this project.

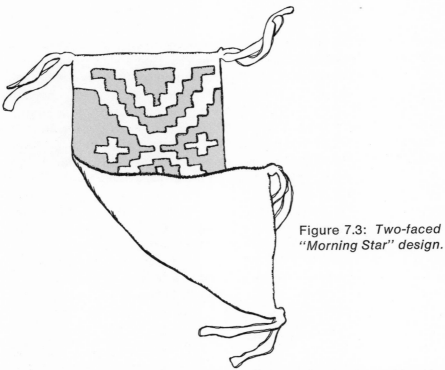

Figure 7.3: *Two-faced
"Morning Star" design.*

In selecting colors for the back side, one important consideration is that they be muted, so the flecks that show to the front will be negligible.

II. *Warping particulars*

Warps for four-heddle techniques are usually spaced more closely than for regular weave. This is because yarns going over multiple warps settle and pack more than usual. If you contemplate a large project, you might consider spacing warps 12 per inch (6 marks per inch on dowels). If you would like a heavier weave, stay with the usual 8 warps per inch, but use a thicker yarn for weft.

The charted design here produces a 10″ x 18½″ project. It uses 41 marks on dowel no. 1 (¼″ intervals) and 40 marks on dowel no. 2. Nails are 17″ apart on the frame.

III. *Materials needed*

4 additional willow sticks for the four sheds (including a thick ½″ one for the stick shed)
Soft, unpolished cotton string for heddles (8 ply)
50 yd. warp (for 10″ x 20″ size)
Four weft colors, uniformly spun for the front side: 2 oz. fleece black; 2½ oz. red; 1 oz. white; 3 oz. indigo

96

The same overall amount (8 oz.) for the back side of your weaving in
your choice of muted hues
Two 50″ two-ply edging cords — red is suggested.

IV. *Counting the sheds*

The counts for the two-faced technique are given below. Please transfer
them to shed and heddle arrangements according to directions in the two-
faced diamond twill project preceding.

STICK SHED AND HEDDLE COUNT FOR THE TWO-FACED TECHNIQUE
(X) = insert batten under these warps

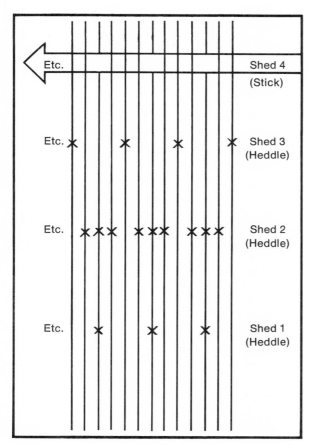

Shed 4
(Stick)

Count: over 1; under 3
Insert batten over 1 and under 3 for entire row noting
exceptions where the row
begins "under 2" and ends
"over 2."

Shed 3
(Heddle)

Count: under 1; over 3
Insert batten under 1 and
then over 3 for the row. Each
"under 1" centers directly
below the "under 3" in the
shed above. Row ends "over
3."

Shed 2
(Heddle)

Count: over 1; under 3
Insert batten over 1 and under 3 for the row. Note that
the "over 1" centers directly
below the "under 1" in the
previous shed, and that
these two sheds are oppo-
site. Row ends "under 3."

Shed 1
(Heddle)

Count: under 1; over 3
Insert batten under 1 and
over 3 for the row. Note that
the "under 1" is directly below the center warp in the 3
count above. Note too that
this shed is opposite shed 4.
The row begins "over 2" and
ends "under 2."

Figure 7.4: *Warp count for the two-faced technique.*
(X) = insert batten behind these warps.

UNDERSTANDING THE TWO-FACED TECHNIQUE

If you will study the shed counts on the preceding page, you will see that sheds 1 and 3 put most of the yarn on the front side of the weaving — yarn goes "over 3" except for an occasional "under 1." The opposite is true of sheds 2 and 4, where most of the yarn skips along the back side, only occasionally latching onto a warp.

With some thought you can see that a white yarn in shed 1 will appear as long stitches on the front side, while the back shows small occasional stitches. A grey yarn following in shed 2 will then slide down *behind* the white to cover those small white stitches on the back. This "a-yarn-for-the-front, a-yarn-for-the-back" rhythm causes the sheds to work in pairs. Shed 1 alternates with 2; shed 3 with 4. Of these, the first is the front yarn; the second is the back.

There is one final concept integral to understanding the workings of the two-faced. Since sheds 1 and 3 control the front side, and since in both cases only every fourth warp comes forward, then it follows that only half the usual number of warps will ever be in the forward position. This further means that designs must be simpler, for turning warps are farther apart.

I. *The chart*

To help clarify the above concept please look at Figure 7.5 that follows. You will note that only half the usual number of warps that cross the batten have been drawn. Since there are 80 warps in all and 20 have been drawn, only one-fourth the total amount ever come forward or can be used as turning warps. Additionally, alternate lines are dark to mark the warps that come forward in shed 1. Light lines denote front warps in shed 3.

As with other turning-joint techniques, all warp threads are counted and turning warps indicated numerically. TW-28L indicates that your "turning warp" is the 28th warp in from the left side of your weaving; TW-27R is the 27th on the right side.

II. *General weaving instructions for the two-faced*

If the concepts described above seem hazy, don't panic! They will clarify with application. Once sheds are in place prepare to weave. Please keep in mind that this is a four-shed technique and that some of the same principles apply as in the twill. Again, it is very important to lay weft in loosely as the two-faced technique consumes enormous amounts of yarn. Also, be certain to keep warps evenly distributed; once again there will be no fill-ins. And finally, the special circling of edge warps in the twill is also encountered here. If any of these principles need review, please reread the appropriate sections in the Two-Faced Diamond Twill.

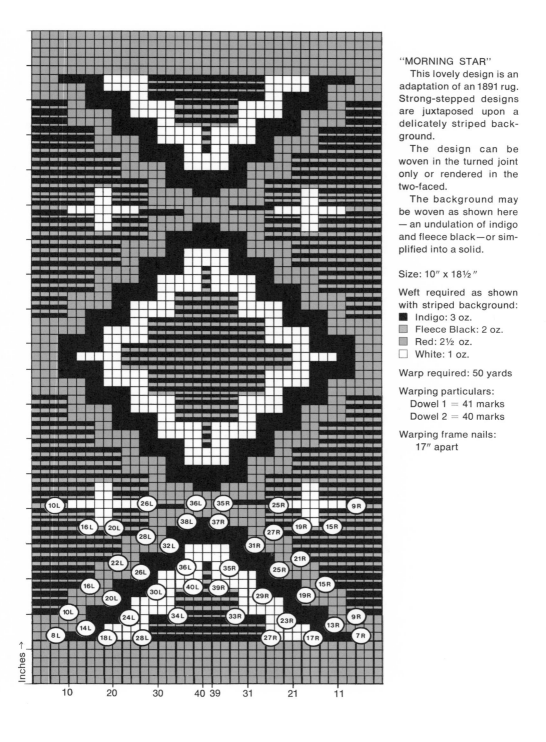

"MORNING STAR"

This lovely design is an adaptation of an 1891 rug. Strong-stepped designs are juxtaposed upon a delicately striped background.

The design can be woven in the turned joint only or rendered in the two-faced.

The background may be woven as shown here — an undulation of indigo and fleece black — or simplified into a solid.

Size: 10″ x 18½″

Weft required as shown with striped background:
■ Indigo: 3 oz.
▦ Fleece Black: 2 oz.
▨ Red: 2½ oz.
□ White: 1 oz.

Warp required: 50 yards

Warping particulars:
Dowel 1 = 41 marks
Dowel 2 = 40 marks

Warping frame nails:
17″ apart

Figure 7.5: *"Morning Star" design charted.*

III. *Specific weaving instructions for the two-faced*

Begin the first four rows of your weaving as usual, taking your yarn in front of the first knot and then under 2, over 2 for the rest of the row.

After these four rows you will begin using your sheds. The order will be 1, 2, 3, 4 repeating, and red will be used in sheds 1 and 3 (front) while your background color will be in alternate sheds.

In using your sheds, simply place batten directly beneath the heddles and then push willows up as far as possible. You will find that when the batten is in shed 2, both heddles 1 and 2 can slide up over it. This is as it should be.

When your weaving is 1¼″ and your red yarn at the right, it is time to begin your design!

A. Morning Star design: Your turning warps are 8L, 18L, 28L, 27R, 17R 7R

Row 1: SHED 1 ←

As you follow directions please refer to Figure 7.5 so you can continue on your own once directions end. Note that the counts in each design area are determined by the number of warps that are forward in that shed. Since this is shed 1, count the number of *dark* warps to determine your count. Lay in your design yarns beginning on your left:

1. Red behind 2 front warps.
2. Black behind next 3.
3. White behind 3 front warps. The last one overlaps the black.
4. Black behind 7 front.
5. White behind 3 front, overlapping last black.
6. Black behind 3.
7. Red behind 2 — again overlapping last black.

Row 2: SHED 2 ←

Back-side yarn goes in shed and slides down behind previous yarns described above.

Row 3: SHED 3 →

Read your chart along with directions, counting the *light* warps in each design area, as this is the third shed. Then lay in your yarns in the following order using directions below:

7. Two	6. Three	5. Three	4. Seven	3. Three	2. Three	1. Two
red	black	white	black	white	black	red

1. Red enters shed and goes to right edge. (TW-7R is behind batten. As per turned-joint rule; ignore it.)

2. Black goes around behind TW-17R and into shed. (TW in front of batten. As per turned-joint rule; include it.) Black goes behind 3 front warps, coming out to the right of TW-7R (TW in front, include).

3. White goes into shed and behind 3 warps (TW-27R in back; ignore). Comes out on top of black yarn to right of TW-17R (TW in front; include).

4. Black goes around behind TW-28L and into shed (TW in front; include). Goes behind 7 front warps and out before white (TW-17R is behind batten; ignore).

5. White goes into shed (TW-18R behind; ignore). Goes behind 3 warps and out on *top of black* to right of 18L (TW-18L in front; include).

This is an especially important row, for it reviews the turning warp rules and the circling of edge warps. If you found it confusing, perhaps you should take it out and put it in again, thinking along with each step. Once again, if you find you are unsure of certain techniques, just review detailed instructions for them in their own chapters.

Row 4: SHED 4 →

Back-side color slides down behind previous design yarns.

Row 5. SHED 1← (begin with yarn on your left)

1. Red two.
2. Black around behind 3 warps, including TW-18L (TW-8L in back; ignore).
3. White behind 3 (include front TW).
4. Black around behind 27R and under 7 (ignore back TW-28L).
5. White behind three (include front TW-27R).
6. Black around behind TW-7R. Three warps.
7. Red two.

Row 6: SHED 2 →

Back-side color slides down behind previous row.

Row 7: SHED 3 ←

Repeat rows 3 through 6 until your pattern is ¼″ high and yarns are at right. Then change your design count as follows:

B. Changing your design count: 14L, 18L, 28L, 27R, 17R, 13R

Shed 1. Follow directions for row 5 above, except bring last yarn 1 warp further. Since your new turning warp (13R) is in back, you can't include it in this row.

Shed 2. As per row 6 above.

Shed 3. As per row 3 above, except:

1. Red goes around behind 13R and then to R edge.

2. Black goes behind 2 only which includes new TW-13R, as it is in front of the batten.

7. Red behind three. New TW (14L) is in back; ignore.

You are now on your own.

As you weave upward, finishing will await you and proceed much as usual. Umbrella ribs are especially helpful here as weft crosses the entire weaving. Keep each heddle in until no longer useful. As each is removed, you will be using a sacking needle to finish your rug. You can refer to the count chart as needed for the threading sequence, ultimately committing the count to memory.

When a novice once groaned aloud that it must be next to impossible to finish a rug in this manner, one Navajo-Weaver-Friend replied calmly to the contrary. "It is at the end," she explained, "that you learn the count by heart — never to forget it." And after some thought, she added, "And at the Moment-of-Knowing This-Kind-of-Weaving belongs to you."

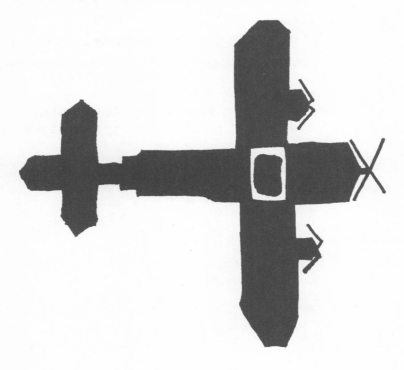

CHAPTER 8

Design Your Own!

PART OF THE PLEASURE the Navajo weaver derives from her art is trying out various designs — ones she's seen her mother and grandmother carry out with such ease and beauty, and now feels ready to attempt on her own. Traditionally designs and their corresponding warp counts are passed down through generations, and a feeling for proportion develops from watching and weaving. Additionally, there is much "on the spot" designing that takes place in the course of the project. For these weavers, then, there is no need to draw a design prior to weaving.

There are others of us, however, who are just learning the craft — who have not had the benefits of observing mothers and grandmothers — who are attempting complex designs early in our Navajo weaving career. For these weavers, it is often helpful to chart designs on paper before the actual weaving begins.

Charting provides many benefits. One can see how shapes and colors will look together and make adjustment at a time that changing the design is easy. One can count the number of warps each shape will need and the distance it should be woven, so that the design will come out right at the center and at the end. And finally, charting a design provides the weaver with a method of computing the amounts of warp and weft that the project requires so that she can weave in peace knowing that colors will not run out prematurely.

If charting a weaving is appropriate to your stage of weaving, here are additional thoughts: *Do a lot of planning!* One rule of thumb is that as much *thought* should precede the project as the time it takes to execute it — and in Navajo weaving that's significant! Additionally, over the years one begins to realize that it takes as much time to weave a beautifully designed rug as it does to weave a poorly designed one. And even more alarming, the amount of time it takes to plan and weave a rug is insignificant to the time that goes into the enjoyment (or dissatisfaction) of it after it is completed!

YEI, YEIBICHEII, SANDPAINTING DESIGNS

In planning the project you are about to weave, you will want to design one appropriate to your present level of ability. Perhaps the ideas in Chapter 1 will be of help. Additionally, you may want to interact with a pattern that has long intrigued you, be it Two Grey Hills, Storm or Crystal. The design ideas in our book list may provide a guide. As you embark on your quest for the next design to form on your loom, there is but one precaution we ask that you carry with you.

Some of the most interesting designs that appear in Navajo rugs are the Yei figures. A line of them, reputedly from the feather dance, face forward, bedecked with ceremonial costuming. Holding rattles and spruce boughs, strings of feathers hang from their elbows. Then, encircling the whole, a Rainbow God wraps itself around the group, bringing promise of a gentle, growing rain.

• Outsiders to the culture see the Yei simply as an appealing pattern, lovely to look at — a challenge to weave. Yet the significance far exceeds these surface qualities. The Yei, Yeibicheii and Sandpainting rugs are all concerned with Navajo ceremony and healing. They are filled with weaving taboos which require ceremonies for protection of the weaver. For this reason, it is strongly suggested that these particular patterns be left for Navajo weavers exclusively. •

If your energies are yet going in this direction and you find it hard to relinquish the pattern, be consoled that there are many beautiful patterns to weave that do not infringe upon a culture or a people's beliefs. If still you find these patterns difficult to ignore, reading about them may satisfy your fascination. Please consult the book list for sources that will deepen your understanding and appreciation of Navajo philosophy and culture.

Some design principles

For those of you who would like to achieve a Navajo feeling to your original design, here are some *basic* designing principles. Based on Navajo life, they underly most rugs.

A. Color

The palette that a weaver selects will determine the feeling of the rug to a large extent. In plant-dyed rugs, colors are largely determined by which plants are available locally — and how easily they are procured and processed. *The most available colors are used for backgrounds and large design areas, whereas difficult, and hence highly prized, colors are savored in small amounts.* As a result, whites, greys and blacks are often a major part of a rug. Of secondary frequency are clear and dull yellows (rabbitbush, for example), and mustards to dull oranges (wild carrot). Greens (sagebrush) are perhaps next frequent, and last are the deep rusts (mountain mahogany), rose hues (prickly pear), and blues (indigo). These *difficult* dyes, when present, are usually in small proportion to the rest of the weaving.

B. Value (darkness and lightness)

When you are selecting your colors give thought not only to the overall look, but also to how they will be placed next to each other. Here value comes into play. To Navajo weavers the darkness or lightness of a color is important. Perhaps evolved over years of weaving in the hoghan without electric lighting, *most Navajo rugs show good contrast.* When weavers work at night by Coleman or kerosene lamp, mistakes often result. Close colors are mistakenly interchanged, and the morning light may reveal such irregularities as bright yellow streaks in dull yellow design. Though impossible to document, it has been my thought that the poor lighting conditions and the resulting mistakes over the years is the *practical* basis for the sometimes-expressed Navajo taboo on night weaving.

C. Design relationship

As a final consideration, if you are designing a rug with a patterned border, give thought to incorporating elements from the interior into the edge. As one weaver expressed, "The two should look like they belong." An example of this is the Greek Key design with the ornate border in Chapter 2.

Once you are aware of the principle, you can browse Navajo rugs, noting how the interior pattern has been adapted to the border. The visual relationship between the two can be most satisfying.

Charting your design

When charting your design, draw it the actual size it will be woven, so you can get an accurate feeling for proportion. Use ruled graph paper with four lines to the inch, so that each ruling on the graph paper will represent one warp as it crosses the batten during counting (p. 46 WWW). By taping the graph papers together, you can see your design in the actual scale it will be woven.

A. Vertical lines of your design

If you will be using the hooked joint in which wefts join *between* warps (diagram, p. 96 WWW), draw your vertical lines between the rulings in your graph paper (see Figure 8.1).

Figure 8.1: *Charting the hooked joint.*

If you will be using the turned joint in which wefts share a single warp (diagram, p. 96 WWW), draw your vertical lines *on* the rulings (see Figure 8.2).

In drawing a design, a beginner should allow at least two warps for a shape. Less than this is difficult for the novice to weave well.

Figure 8.2: *Charting the turned joint.*

B. Horizontal lines of your design

Draw your horizontal lines *on* the rulings of your graph paper. This will facilitate measuring at a future time. Each square will represent ¼" of weaving. Four squares will equal one inch of weaving.

C. Diagonal lines of your design

Weaving will be easier if diagonals are consistently angled. For the 45-degree angle, step your design diagonally one square high and one square wide. For the shallower angle, slant your diagonal one square high to *two* squares wide. In the actual weaving, your achievement of these angles will depend on your warp/weft ratio and on your packing. If you are using the hooked joint, simply weave in place ¼″ and then side-step one full warp (¼″) that crosses the batten. This will give you the 45-degree angle (see Figures 8.3 and 8.4).

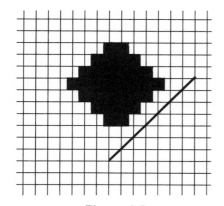

Figure 8.3:
Charting the stepped diagonal.

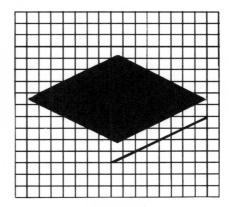

Figure 8.4:
Charting the smooth diagonal.

For the shallower angle it is best to use the turned joint. Here stepping can be *an individual warp to the side,* or for an even shallower angle, two individual warps. If you want a steeper angle, then consider the serrated edge or the hooked joint with its stepped edge (diagram, p. 98 WWW).

How to estimate overall quantities of weft

Navajo weavers do not pre-draw their designs, nor do they calculate amounts of yarns. They simply look at what they have, and estimate whether it is sufficient for what they have in mind. Once again, repetition over generations plays a substantial part in their accuracy.

Some minds are good at estimating. Some are not. For some people, running out of yarn prior to finishing simply means an adjustment is in order. For others it is a catastrophe!

If you are of the latter variety, the following procedure can be used to compute, rather than to guess at, yarn quantities. (Some people enjoy estimating and then comparing it with the mathematical approach.)

A. Procedure for computation

1. Compute total number of square inches in your project. (Multiply length of rug by width in inches.)

(width in inches) $\times$ (length in inches) = (total square inches)

107

2. To determine the total amount of weft you will need, apply whichever formula below is appropriate.

a. *If your project has less than 1000 sq. inches, one ounce of weft will cover 25 sq. inches.*

(no. of sq. inches under 1000) ÷ 25 = (total weft in ounces)

b. *If your project has more than 1000 sq. inches, one ounce of weft will cover 30 sq. inches.*

(no. of sq. inches over 1000) ÷ 30 = (total weft in ounces)

When you have determined the total square inches and the total weft needed, compare both with the chart below. This is to affirm that you are in the right "ball park." If figures are significantly different, compute again, slowly and carefully. Get a friend to help if necessary. If no one is available, try talking it aloud to yourself.

APPROXIMATE WARP AND WEFT QUANTITIES		
Size of Project (length × width, in inches)	Amount of Warp Needed	Approximate Amount of Weft Needed
225 square inches	50 yards +	½ lb. +
450 square inches	100 yards +	1 lb. +
675 square inches	150 yards +	1½ lb. +
900 square inches	200 yards +	2 lb. +
1125 square inches	250 yards +	2½ lb. +
1350 square inches	300 yards +	3 lb. +
1575 square inches	350 yards +	3½ lb. +
1800 square inches	400 yards +	4 lb. +

B. Qualifications and additional considerations

1. Always over-order rather than order too little. Colors are often hard to match, and frustrations build while waiting for a second shipment.

2. Estimates above are based on rugs in which weft is firmly packed and warp turns are ¼" apart (8 per inch).

How to compute quantities of each yarn color

Once the overall estimate is obtained you may want to guess at how it is distributed among colors (i.e. half for the background, a fourth for the main design, an eighth for the border, etc.). However, if you would still like to be certain when you order colors, you can continue with more mathematical formulae!

1. Draw your design on graph paper and color it in.

108

2. Determine the number of ¼" squares in entire project. (Either multiply number of squares in length by those in width, or multiply total square inches (from previous page) by 16. The two should match. Write this number here:_____(total number of ¼" squares).

3. Count number of ¼" squares of each color. Count two half-squares as one whole one. Record amounts below:

Color	Number of Squares
_____	_____
_____	_____
_____	_____
_____	_____

4. Once again, the size of the project determines the formula to apply. Write the appropriate numbers below.

If project is under 1000 square inches and one ounce covers 25 square inches, then *one ounce* will also cover *400 squares.*

If project size is over 1000 square inches and one ounce covers 30 square inches, then one ounce will also cover *480 squares.*

Color	Number of Squares		400 or 480		Yarn Needed in Ounces
_____	_____	×	_____	=	_____
_____	_____	×	_____	=	_____
_____	_____	×	_____	=	_____
_____	_____	×	_____	=	_____
Total_____				Total_____	

Compare your totals here with your previously calculated number of squares in project and amount of yarn needed.

How to estimate quantity of warp needed

Using the formula below compute your warp:

(width of weaving in inches) × (number of individual warps per inch*)
× (length of weaving in inches) = (total warp needed in inches)

(warp needed in inches — from above) ÷ 36 (inches in a yard)
= (total yards of warp needed)

Please compare this amount with previous chart.

---

* If you are using ¼" graph paper and plan on marking dowels at ¼" intervals (4 marks per inch) your number will be 8.

How to use your chart in weaving

1. You can now use your chart to help you in warping: Just count the total number of vertical lines in your chart. This number represents your "warp turns" in a weaving of that width.

Make that number of marks on dowel no. 2.

Add one more mark to dowel no. 1.

2. You can use your chart to tell you how many warps each design will be — just count the vertical rulings within each colored area.

3. You can use your chart to tell you how far you should weave in place before changing that warp count. Count your squares upward. Each one equals ¼″ of weaving and four equal 1″.

4. You can use your chart to tell you the angle on your diagonal joint and what joint to use. For a 45-degree angle, use the hooked joint, weaving your yarn in place for ¼″ and then side-stepping one full warp in front of the batten. For shallower than the 45 degree, use the turned joint, sidestepping an individual warp with each row.

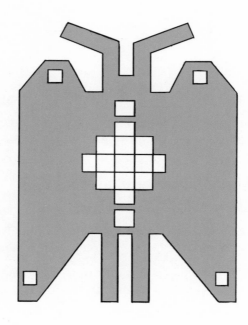

Suggested Reading

IF YOU'RE TIRED of weaving but not of dreaming . . .

If you're looking for inspiration on your next weaving . . .

If you've run out of yarn and find it difficult to await replacement, then perhaps this reading guide can help you through.

Book lists

FOR DESIGN IDEAS OF GENERAL PATTERNS

Arizona Highways. July, 1974. This issue is dedicated exclusively to Navajo rugs and contains over 75 good color photographs and 2 pictures of large lumber-made looms.

Navajo Rugs — How to Find, Evaluate, Buy and Care for Them, Don Dedera. Northland Press, 1975. Rug photos include 36 color; 28 black and white. Some old rugs included and large lumber looms pictured pp. 22, 92.

Navajo Rugs — Past, Present and Future, Gilbert Maxwell. 1963. Small publication with 20 small color and 15 black-and-white reproductions of rugs.

Navajo Textiles — From the Read Mullen Collection. The Heard Museum, 1976. More than 50 large color photos of quality rugs.

Ray Manley's Southwest Indian Arts and Crafts. The section on Navajo rugs contains 47 large quality color photographs and 2 pictures of traditional looms.

FOR DESIGN IDEAS OF PICTORIAL PATTERNS

American Indian Art, "Navajo Pictorial Weaving," Charlene Cerny. Winter, 1976. 5 color, 2 black and white.

Arizona Highways. July, 1976. Large welded pipe loom on cover, lumber loom p. 15. Story on weaving of bicentennial flag rugs.

Navajo Pictorial Weaving, Charlene Cerny. Museum of New Mexico, 1975. Five color, 20 black-and-white photos.

DESIGN IDEAS OF OLD RUGS

American Indian Art, Scottsdale, Arizona. This quality periodical contains lovely photographs of rare old rugs, especially in advertisements.

Between Traditions — Navajo Weaving toward the End of the Nineteenth Century, J. J. Brody. University of Iowa Museum of Art, 1976.

Indian Blankets and their Makers, George Wharton James, 1914. Rio Grande Classic Reprint, 1937. This lovely old book preserves some of the most attractive simple old rug designs. Thirty-one color photos; 58 black and white. Loom illustrations: pp. 103, 104, 107, 145.

The Navajo and His Blanket, U. S. Hollister, 1903. Rio Grande Press Classic Reprint, 1972.

Walk in Beauty: The Navajo and Their Blankets, Berlant and Kahlenberg, New York Graphic Society, 1977. Beautiful old designs.

Navajo Textile Arts, H. P. Mera. Originally published in the late 1930s as a series of small articles by the Laboratory of Anthropology in Santa Fe, this has been reprinted by Peregrine Smith, 1975. Almost 100 black-and-white photographs of old rugs.

Patterns and Sources of Navajo Weaving, Harmsen's Western Americana Collection, 1977.

The Story of Navajo Weaving, Kate Peck Kent. Heard Museum, 1961. This softcover book contains 34 large color photographs. A large log loom is pictured on the cover.

The previously listed books have been cited solely for their photographs. Unfortunately, much of what is *written* about Navajo culture and weaving is erroneous, taken from traders and sources outside the culture itself. In subsequent writings these works are often quoted, thereby propagating the mistruths. Since it is impossible for the uninformed to differentiate between accurate and inaccurate "facts," and since it is also difficult to rid the mind of what has been taken in, I recommend reading only sources whose material is taken from the Navajo directly. The following list of recommended reading stresses *accuracy:*

FOR WEAVING PHILOSOPHY AND A FEELING FOR THE PEOPLE

Any of Reichard's books are recommended. Gladys Reichard was an anthropologist who spent summers living with Navajo families and learning weaving. She was a keen observer with a gifted mind, independent spirit, and caring soul. From my viewpoint, her books are always fascinating *and* accurate — a rare combination!

Navaho Shepherd and Weaver, Gladys Reichard. Originally printed in 1936. Reprinted Rio Grande Press, 1900. This is the best beginning book to read, containing a fascinating account of her on-and-off loom experiences during the 1930s in a day when the reservation was much less developed.

Spiderwoman — A Story of Navajo Weavers and Chanters. Gladys Reichard, 1934. This is recommended as a second book to enjoy. Concerned less with weaving, this book goes further into ceremonial ways and beliefs.

The Weaver's Pathway — A Clarification of the "Spirit Trail" in Navajo Weaving, Noël Bennett. Northland Press, 1974. This book is dedicated to accurately communicating the meaning of the small line extending through borders of some Navajo rugs. Its intent is to dispel long-associated myths and open up the real beauty of accompanying thought.

ACCURATE INFORMATION ON CARE AND SELECTION OF RUGS

A Consumer's Guide to Southwestern Indian Arts and Crafts, Mark Bahti, 1975. This booklet gives a good idea of what to look for when purchasing all types of Indian crafts, and how to distinguish the real from the fake. Mark Bahti upholds his father's commitment to quality merchandise, accurate representation, and concern for Indian problems.

Genuine Navajo Rug — Are You Sure???, Noël Bennett. The Navajo Tribe and The Museum of Navajo Ceremonial Art, 1973. This booklet offers a clear method of distinguishing between real Navajo rugs and their Mexican imitations. Information contained herein has been summarized as a final chapter in *Navajo Weaving Handbook,* Museum of New Mexico Press, 1977.

FOR GENERAL UNDERSTANDING OF THE NAVAJO WAY

The Enduring Navaho, Laura Gilpin. University of Texas Press, 1968. A beautiful pictorial presentation of old photos that capture the essence of the traditional way.

Song of the Earth Spirit, Susan Anderson. Friends of the Earth, 1974.

Hosteen Klah — Navaho Medicine Man and Sand Painter, Franc Newcomb. University of Oklahoma, 1965. A highly readable account of a famous medicine man and weaver.

FOR ACCURATE IN-DEPTH UNDERSTANDING

Navajo Religion: A Study of Symbolism, Gladys Reichard. Vols. I and II, 1950. An heroic compilation of Navajo beliefs in all areas.

An Ethnologic Dictionary of the Navaho Language, Berard Haile, 1910. Father Berard Haile of the Franciscan order, Saint Michaels, Arizona, was another very perceptive observer and recorder. His prolific writings span many subjects. Some are highly technical and the reader's appreciation and comprehension is heightened by bringing some background to the subject. The chapter on weaving included in this particular work records a very traditional and vanishing approach.

Some Sex Beliefs and Practices in a Navaho Community, Flora Bailey. Peabody Museum of American Archaeology and Ethnology, Harvard University, Vol. XL-No. 2, 1950. This is a well-researched report on taboos and beliefs that underly many areas of the Navajo way. Interesting weaving taboos included in such areas as pregnancy and childbirth — all of which have been substantiated in my experience on reservation.

FOR RESEARCHERS

For people who are doing research on *recorded* Navajo weaving, we refer you to a most valuable aide:

Navajo Bibliography with Subject Index, Revised Edition, Correll, Watson, Brugge. Research Report No. 2, Research Section, Navajo Parks and Recreation, The Navajo Tribe, Window Rock, Arizona, 1969. Included here are books, newspaper articles, and unpublished theses — "all available references to the Navaho People, their land and environment, regardless of source and without attempt to evaluate." Approximately 150 of these listings deal with Navajo weaving *per se.* (See "Weaving" and "Arts and Crafts" as subject headings.) One cannot be confronted by this project without being struck at the enormity of the undertaking.

Glossary of Terms

ANILINE DYES: Chemically compounded, synthetic organic dyes. These are commercially prepared, powdered dyes sold to weavers at the trading posts.

BATTEN: A flattened, smoothed wooden tool used to keep the shed open while a weft is inserted.

BOWLINE KNOT: An effective warping knot used to secure beginning and end of warp so that during weaving, knots will not slip under downward fork pressure. The bowline is also useful in repairing a broken warp.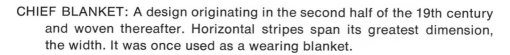

CHIEF BLANKET: A design originating in the second half of the 19th century and woven thereafter. Horizontal stripes span its greatest dimension, the width. It was once used as a wearing blanket.

COAL-MINE RAISED EDGE: Typically a rug woven near Coal-Mine Mesa (western Navajo reservation) with vertical pin stripes permeating designs with raised outlines.

CRYSTAL: Typically a rug woven in the Crystal area (eastern Navajo reservation) of plant dyed yarns in which stripes of wavy lines alternate with other designs.

DIAMOND TWILL: Typically saddle blankets woven with four sheds to create tri-colored diamonds of varying sizes. Both sides of the rug have the same colors and designs, but each bears a different color emphasis.

EDGING AND SELVAGE CORD: Two-ply yarn used on edges of weaving in selvage position. For distinguishing purposes, "edging cord" refers to the binding at the top and bottom while "selvage cord" pertains to that on the sides.

GANADO: Typically a rug woven in the Ganado area (central Navajo reservation) and characterized by a deep red aniline background.

HEDDLE ROD: A device used to create the pull shed. A stick is placed horizontally in front of the warps. String is looped from it to those warps which are in back position in the stick shed. When the heddle rod is pulled, these back warps can be brought forward to create an alternate shed.

HOOKED JOINT (interlocking weft): A method of forming designs so as to prevent a slit between colors. Here adjoining wefts hook together before entering the next shed. This hook occurrs between warps, and the line created is straight (unserrated). No build-up occurs where the vertical is maintained as in a border.

INVERSION TECHNIQUE: A way of finishing ornately bordered rugs in their more simplified center, to ease the tedious end-rug weaving.

"LAZY-LINE": A faintly visible line of pinholes that diagonally transverse a plain area — resulting from that area being woven in sections. More aptly called "sectional weaving line."

PICTORIAL: Typically a rug woven on the eastern side of the reservation which depicts aspects of reservation life or other designs of interest to the weaver.

PLANT DYES: Natural dyes extracted from local plants.

PULL SHED: An opening between front and back warps created by separating the two shed rods, and pulling on the heddle rod. In this manner, the back warps are brought into a forward position. A batten is inserted and a weft may be passed.

116

SADDLE BLANKET: Typically rather thick, bordered weavings without center design which are used beneath the saddle. Overall diamond twills are also prevalent. The usual single saddle blanket size is 30″ x 30″, the double, 30″ x 60″.

SCALLOPS OR BUBBLING: A means of laying weft loosely into a shed so as to control the weft tension.

SHED: The opening between front and back warps through which a weft is passed. The shed is created by manipulation of rods and held open by the batten turned on edge.

SHED ROD: A stick passed behind alternate warps for the purpose of holding every other warp forward, and creating the opening into which a batten may be inserted for the stick shed.

SQUARE KNOT: The basic knot used in Navajo weaving, made with two ends as follows:
    Left over right, around and through.
    Right over left, around and through.

STICK SHED: An opening between front and back warps created by positioning the shed and heddle rods together. A batten, inserted below the rods, holds the warps apart for passage of a weft.

STICK-SHUTTLE: A dry straight twig on which weft is wrapped, and by means of which weft is carried through the shed from side to side in areas of solid stripe.

STORM PATTERN: Typically a rug woven in the Tuba City area (western Navajo reservation) in black, white, grey and red with "storm pattern" symbols.

TAPESTRY WEAVE: The most common Navajo weave created by two sheds in which wefts go over and under successive warps to completely cover them.

TUFTING: The weaving-in of long goat hair tufts to create a fleece effect.

TURNED JOINT (interlocking warp): A method of forming design so as to prevent a slit between colors. Here adjoining wefts turn around the same warp before entering the next shed. On a vertical design edge, this dovetailing produces a serrated effect. Build-up occurs when the vertical is maintained as in a border. On a diagonal design edge the result is a smooth, gradual line.

TURNING WARP: The common warp shared by adjoining wefts in creating a turned joint design.

TWO-FACED: Typically a two-sided weaving with a designed front and a striped back. Made with four sheds, this weaving is thicker than usual and each side can have entirely different designs and colors.

TWO-FACED DIAMOND TWILL: A combination of Two-Faced and Diamond Twill techniques, also rendered in four sheds. Stripes of variegated diamonds outline blocks of solid color, one on the front, a different color on the back.

TWO GREY HILLS: Typically a rug woven in the Two Grey Hills area (eastern Navajo reservation) of fine yarns in natural fleece hues.

UP-AND-OVER TECHNIQUE: A method of attaching long warp to a short loom. Warp is stretched from loom base, up and over top beam, to the rope tensioning arrangement which is in the back.

WARP: The thin, tightly spun yarn initially stretched on the loom in preparation for the actual weaving.

WEFT: The thicker, softer spun yarn woven over and under warps and from side to side to create design.

YEI RUG: Typically a rug woven on the eastern side of the Navajo reservation depicting forward-facing feather dancers with a rainbow figure encircling sides and bottom.